JN089228

STEP-UP SKILLS FOR THE TOEIC®
L&R TEST: Level 4 —Mastery—

Yasuyuki Kitao

Harumi Nishida

Shiho Hayashi

Brian Covert

Asahi Press

音声再生アプリ「リスニング・トレーナー」を使った音声ダウンロード

朝日出版社開発のアプリ、「リスニング・トレーナー（リストレ）」を使えば、教科書の音声をスマホ、タブレットに簡単にダウンロードできます。どうぞご活用ください。

◉ アプリ【リスニング・トレーナー】の使い方

《アプリのダウンロード》

App Store または Google Play から「リスニング・トレーナー」のアプリ（無料）をダウンロード

App Storeは
こちら▶

Google Playは
こちら▶

《アプリの使い方》

① アプリを開き「コンテンツを追加」をタップ
② 画面上部に【15720】を入力しDoneをタップ

音声ストリーミング配信 》》》

この教科書の音声は、右記ウェブサイトにて無料で配信しています。

https://text.asahipress.com/free/english/

協力
株式会社リント

■ はじめに

TOEIC®（Test of English for International Communication）テストは、「世界共通語としての英語によるコミュニケーション能力を測定するテスト」として、世界最大のテスト開発機関 ETS（Educational Testing Service）によって開発され、1979年12月に第1回公開試験が実施されました。英語の聞く力・読む力・文法の知識を測るリスニングとリーディングを中心とする試験でしたが、2007年には英語を話す力・書く力を測る TOEIC® SPEAKING AND WRITING TESTS が始まり、今では英語の4技能（聞く・読む・話す・書く）の力を測ることができるテストになっています。また TOEIC® という名称は、以前は昔からあったリスニングとリーディングのテストを指していましたが、2016年8月からは、英語の聞く力・読む力を測るテストである TOEIC® LISTENING AND READING TEST（略称：TOEIC® L&R）と、英語の話す力・書く力を測る TOEIC® SPEAKING AND WRITING TESTS（略称：TOEIC® S&W）の両方を指すテストブランド名として用いられることになりました。このことからも、TOEIC® テストは、英語の4技能を測るテストへと進化し続けていることがよく分かります。

　本テキストでは、これまでに朝日出版社より出版した『一歩上を目指す TOEIC® LISTENING AND READING TEST』シリーズをベースに、より高い難易度のテキスト作りを目指しました。これは、出版社に届いていた「Level 3 —Advanced—」よりも高いレベルのテキストを求める声に応えたものです。

　Level 4 —Mastery—では、一部、実際の TOEIC® L&R で出てくる語彙よりも難易度の高い語彙を用いています。これは、本テキストは単に TOEIC® L&R の対策だけを目指すものではなく、TOEIC® L&R に即した問題を解く中で、より高い英語力を身につけてもらうことを目指しているためです。

　本テキストには、TOEIC® L&R の Part 1 から Part 7 の形式の問題に加えて、語彙問題（Vocabulary）および文法解説（Grammar）を取り入れました。語彙問題は、日本語を介さずに英文から語彙を選ぶ方式にしています。これにより、文の中で語の意味を理解しながら語彙力をつけてもらうこと、および前後関係から意味を探り出す力を身につけることを目指しています。文法解説は、文法を公式として捉えるのではなく、テーマに挙げた文法項目の考え方を理解してもらうことを目指しています。解説を熟読し、例文を参考にして、英語の文に伴う文法の感覚を養ってほしいと思います。

　本テキストを隅から隅まで活用していただくことにより、皆さんの英語の知識が増え、英語の聞く力・読む力が向上し、併せて TOEIC® L&R のスコアが向上すれば、これに勝る喜びはありません。

　本書を刊行するにあたっては、朝日出版社第一編集部の朝日英一郎様と鹿糖晟人様にたいへんお世話になりました。朝日様と鹿糖様のきめ細やかなご配慮および編集面からの的確なコメントにより、本テキストがより良いものになったことは間違いありません。また、他の編集部の皆様にも各段階でたいへんお世話になりました。ここに感謝申し上げます。

2023年10月

著者

■ 本書について

■ 本書の構成

　本書は実際のTOEIC® LISTENING AND READING TEST（以下、TOEIC® L&Rと略）に準拠した問題とともに、語彙の練習問題および文法説明を設けています。TOEIC® L&R形式の問題を解くことに加えて、英語の力を伸ばすことを目標に据えています。

　本書の構成は以下のとおりです。

◆ Vocabulary（語彙問題）
　各ユニットで出てくる重要語句を理解しましょう。

◆ TOEIC® L&R練習問題　Part 1: Photographs（写真描写問題）
　写真を見て英文を聞き、英語を聞く力を身につけましょう。

◆ TOEIC® L&R練習問題　Part 2: Question-Response（応答問題）
　文字情報に頼らず、音声情報だけで英語を聞き取れるようにしましょう。

◆ TOEIC® L&R練習問題　Part 3: Conversation（会話問題）
　会話をとおして英語を聞く力を身につけるとともに、会話でよく使われる表現を身につけましょう。

◆ TOEIC® L&R練習問題　Part 4: Talk（説明文問題）
　説明文を聞き、長い英語を聞き取れるようにしましょう。

◆ Grammar（文法説明）
　文法について、その考え方が詳しく書かれています。英語の構造についての理解を深めましょう。

◆ TOEIC® L&R練習問題　Part 5: Incomplete Sentences（短文穴埋め問題）
　文法問題をとおして、英語の文法や語彙の知識を増やしましょう。

◆ TOEIC® L&R練習問題　Part 6: Text Completion（長文穴埋め問題）
　長文空所補充問題をとおして、英語を読む力を身につけるとともに、文法や語彙の知識を増やしましょう。

◆ TOEIC® L&R練習問題　Part 7: Single Passage（1つの文書）/ Multiple Passages（複数の文書）
　様々な英文テキストを読み、問題に答えることで、英語の読解力を身につけましょう。

■ 本書の使い方

　本書はUnit 1からUnit 14まで14のテーマに基づいて問題が作られています。

　TOEIC® L&R形式のリスニング練習問題（Part 1 ～ Part 4）を解く前に、ボキャブラリーの問題を解いて語彙力の増強を図ってください。またTOEIC® L&R形式のリーディング練習問題（Part 5 ～ Part 7）を解く前に、文法説明をよく読んで、英語の文法の知識を身につけるとともに、英語の感覚を身につけるよう心がけましょう。朝日出版社のウェブページには本テキストのリスニング問題の音声があります。こちらもダウンロードして、ぜひ活用してください（URLは、テキスト「はじめに」のページの前に載せています）。

TOEIC® LISTENING AND READING TESTの形式について

　TOEIC® LISTENING AND READING TEST（TOEIC® L&R）は、リスニング問題100問（45分）、リーディング問題100問（75分）で構成されています。合否を判定するテストではなく、スコアにより評価されます。リスニング、リーディング各セクションが5点から495点の間でスコアとして算出され、2つのセクションを合計した、10点から990点の間でトータルスコアが算出されます。

　TOEIC®を開発・製作しているEducational Testing Service（略称ETS）が、リスニング・リーディングのセクションごとに、スコア別に「長所」(Strength)と「短所」(Weakness)を記したレベル別評価の一覧表「Score Descriptor Table」を発表しています（https://www.ets.org/pdfs/toeic/toeic-listening-reading-score-descriptors.pdf）。日本でのTOEIC®の運営団体である「一般財団法人 国際ビジネスコミュニケーション協会」の公式ウェブページには、この評価一覧表を日本語に訳したものが挙げられています（https://www.iibc-global.org/toeic/test/lr/guide04/guide04_02/score_descriptor.html）。これらを自分の英語の力を測る目安として利用するとともに、スコアアップを目指す上での指針にするとよいでしょう。

　TOEIC® L&R TESTは7つのパートに分かれています。そのうち4つのパートがリスニングで、3つのパートがリーディングです。リスニングではアメリカ・カナダ・イギリス・オーストラリア（ニュージーランドを含む）の英語が25％ずつ採用されています。各パートの問題形式および問題数は次のとおりです。

【リスニング セクション】

パート	内容	問題数
Part 1	**Photographs（写真描写問題）** 写真を見て、4つの説明文から写真の内容を最も的確に表現しているものを選びます。選択肢は印刷されていません。	6問
Part 2	**Question-Response（応答問題）** 質問文を聞いて、それに続く3つの応答から質問の答えとして合致しているものを選びます。質問文・応答とも印刷されていません。	25問
Part 3	**Conversations (with and without a visual image)（会話問題）** 2人もしくは3人で行われる会話に関連して出される設問に対して、適切な答えを選びます。1つの会話に対して、3つの質問が出されます。音声情報のみで答える問題もあれば、表やグラフ、地図などが付いた問題もあります。質問文も解答の選択肢もどちらも印刷されています。	39問 〔3問ずつ 13題〕
Part 4	**Talks (with and without a visual image)（説明文問題）** 1人の話者によるアナウンスを聞き、そのアナウンスに関する質問に答えます。音声情報のみで答える問題もあれば、表やグラフ、地図などが付いた問題もあります。質問文、解答の選択肢、両方印刷されています。	30問 〔3問ずつ 10題〕

【リーディング セクション】

パート	内容	問題数
Part 5	**Incomplete Sentences（短文穴埋め問題）** 短文の空所に当てはまる語句を4つの選択肢から選びます。 文法および語彙に関する問題が出題されます。	30問
Part 6	**Text Completion（長文穴埋め問題）** 1つの文章に対して、4つ穴埋めの問題があります。うち3つは単語や句を選ぶ問題で、文法的な見地や語彙の観点から問題が出されます。残り1つは文を補充する問題です。文脈を考えて、適切な文を選択肢より選びます。	16問 〔4問ずつ 4題〕
Part 7	**Single Passage（1つの文書）、Multiple Passages（複数の文書）** 様々な英文テキストから問題が出されます。電子メールなどのテキストメッセージやチャットなど、複数の人物がやり取りしている文章もあります。それぞれのテキストに対して数問問題が出され、各々の質問に対して適切な答えを4つの選択肢から選びます。 1つの文章から問題が出されるSingle Passageの問題と、2つあるいは3つの文章から問題が出されるMultiple Passagesの問題の2つのタイプがあります。	29問 (single) 25問 (multiple)

　TOEIC® LISTENING AND READING TESTの公開テストを受験するには、TOEIC® 公式ウェブページからのインターネット申し込みが必要です。詳しくは下記のTOEIC® 公式ウェブページをご覧ください。

●**TOEIC® 公式ウェブページ（一般財団法人 国際ビジネスコミュニケーション協会）**
https://www.iibc-global.org/toeic.html

　同ウェブページによると、本テキスト執筆時で最新のデータである2022年度のTOEIC® L&Rの受験者数は、公開テスト受験者が97万人、団体特別受験制度による受験者が100万1千人の計197万1千人でした。

TOEIC® Programについて

現在、TOEIC® Programには、以下のテストがあります。

TOEIC® Tests

・TOEIC® LISTENING AND READING TEST
　　英語を聞く力、読む力、および英文法の知識を測るテストです。
　　　　＜テスト形式＞ マークシートによる一斉客観テスト
　　　　＜テスト時間＞ 120分（リスニング 45分、リーディング 75分）
　　　　＜テスト結果＞ リスニング 5 ～ 495 点、リーディング 5 ～ 495 点、
　　　　　　　　　　　合計 10 ～ 990 点
　　　　　　　　　　　（スコアは 5 点刻みで算出されます。）

・TOEIC® SPEAKING AND WRITING TESTS
　　英語を話す力および書く力を測るテストです。
　　　　＜テスト形式＞ テスト会場にてパソコンを使用して実施
　　　　＜テスト時間＞ スピーキング 20分、ライティング 60分
　　　　＜テスト結果＞ スピーキング 0 ～ 200 点、ライティング 0 ～ 200 点、
　　　　　　　　　　　（スコアは 10 点刻みで算出されます。）
　　　　　　　　　　　　　※スピーキングのみ、ライティングのみの受験も可能です。

TOEIC Bridge® Tests

・TOEIC Bridge® Listening & Reading Tests
　　TOEIC® LISTEING AND READING TEST (TOEIC® L&R) よりも易しいレベ
　ルのテストで、英語を聞く力、読む力、および英文法の知識を測るテストです。
　　　　＜テスト形式＞ マークシートによる一斉客観テスト
　　　　＜テスト時間＞ 60分（リスニング 25分、リーディング 35分）
　　　　＜テスト結果＞ リスニング 15 ～ 50 点、リーディング 15 ～ 50 点、
　　　　　　　　　　　合計 30 ～ 100 点
　　　　　　　　　　　（スコアは 1 点刻みで算出されます。）

・TOEIC Bridge® Speaking & Writing Tests
　　TOEIC® SPEAKING AND WRITING TESTS (TOEIC® S&W) よりも易しいレ
　ベルのテストで、英語を話す力および書く力を測るテストです。
　　　　＜テスト形式＞ テスト会場にてパソコンを使用して実施
　　　　＜テスト時間＞ 52分（スピーキング 15分、ライティング 37分）
　　　　＜テスト結果＞ スピーキング 15 ～50 点、ライティング 15 ～ 50 点、
　　　　　　　　　　　合計 30 ～ 100 点
　　　　　　　　　　　（スコアは 1 点刻みで算出されます。）
　　　　※IPテストの場合は、スピーキングのみ、ライティングのみの受験も可能です。

詳しくは、TOEIC® 公式ウェブページをご覧ください。

Contents

STEP-UP SKILLS FOR THE TOEIC®
L&R TEST: Level 4 —Mastery—

Eating Out

Warm-up

Vocabulary

空欄に下から適切な語を選んで書き入れなさい。なお、動詞については原形で記されています。必要に応じて適切な形に変えなさい。

1. The sports organization provided two (　　　　　) tickets per game to players, coaches and full-time staff members.

2. It was a (　　　　　) opportunity to meet, eat and drink with the local people.

3. I hope your words will (　　　　　) him to change his mind.

4. You are required to (　　　　　) the document and insert a signature before using this machine.

5. Only the workers of this building can (　　　　　) at this café and they can put the check on their tab.

6. The cake looks so delicious, but I'm (　　　　　) and don't have room for it.

convince	stuffed	complimentary
review	terrific	dine

TOEIC® Listening

Part 1 Photographs

You will hear four short statements. Look at the picture and choose the statement that best describes what you see in the picture.

1.

Ⓐ Ⓑ Ⓒ Ⓓ

2.
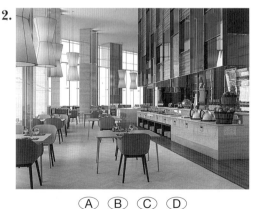

Ⓐ Ⓑ Ⓒ Ⓓ

Part 2 Question-Response

You will hear a question or statement and three responses. Listen carefully, and choose the best response to the question or statement.

3. Mark your answer on your answer sheet.   Ⓐ Ⓑ Ⓒ

4. Mark your answer on your answer sheet.   Ⓐ Ⓑ Ⓒ

5. Mark your answer on your answer sheet.   Ⓐ Ⓑ Ⓒ

6. Mark your answer on your answer sheet.   Ⓐ Ⓑ Ⓒ

Part 3 Conversation

You will hear a short conversation between two or more people. Listen carefully, and select the best response to each question.

7. **What is mentioned about the chocolate mousse pie?**
   (A) It is not on the menu anymore.
   (B) It will be served with ice cream.
   (C) It is today's special.
   (D) It is very popular.   Ⓐ Ⓑ Ⓒ Ⓓ

8. **What does the woman say about the chocolate mousse pie?**
   (A) She wants it with coffee.
   (B) She does not think her friend will like it.
   (C) She had it with her friends before.
   (D) She thinks it sells well.   Ⓐ Ⓑ Ⓒ Ⓓ

9. **What will the server bring next?**
   (A) A bill
   (B) Tea and coffee
   (C) Apple pie with ice cream
   (D) Chocolate mousse pie   Ⓐ Ⓑ Ⓒ Ⓓ

You will hear a short talk given by a single speaker. Listen carefully, and select the best response to each question.

10. **What does the speaker mention about the restaurant?**

    (A) It is expanding to new cities.

    (B) It is having an opening special tonight.

    (C) It is locally owned.

    (D) It is part of a chain.   Ⓐ Ⓑ Ⓒ Ⓓ

11. **Look at the menu. How much is the Giant Rib Rack tonight?**

    (A) $10.99

    (B) $12.99

    (C) $14.99

    (D) $16.99   Ⓐ Ⓑ Ⓒ Ⓓ

12. **What will the server bring next?**

    (A) Alcoholic beverages

    (B) Menus

    (C) Appetizer

    (D) The rib plates   Ⓐ Ⓑ Ⓒ Ⓓ

品詞（その1）

●品詞の見分け方（その1）

＜例題＞　次の下線部に当てはまる語句を記号で選びなさい。
(A) effectiveness　　(B) effective　　(C) effectively

① Building _____ workplace relationships is an extremely important skill for any employee.

② I believe that the department needs more communication to work more _____.

③ Now many companies understand the _____ of online education and have prepared lots of learning programs.

④ The new law will become _____ next month.

⑤ The system was not running as _____ as the instructions suggested.

⑥ The former CEO _____ controls the company.

　TOEIC® L&Rでは、文の空所に当てはまる適切な品詞を選ぶ問題が出ます。意味の面から考えるよりはむしろ、構造から適切な品詞を探り出す術が必要になってきます。品詞の働きを知り、語の感覚を研ぎ澄ませましょう。

　例題①は、空所の後に複合語の名詞句workplace relationshipsがあることに着目する必要があります。空所に入る語は文頭のBuildingを修飾しているのではなく、名詞句workplace relationshipsを修飾しています。名詞を修飾するのは「形容詞」であることから、形容詞の(B) effectiveが答えになります。

　例題②は、空所の語句は空所の前のmoreと結びついて、動詞workを修飾しています。動詞を修飾するのは「副詞」ですので、副詞の(C) effectivelyが答えになります。

　例題③は、空所の前にtheがあり、後にofが来ていることから、theとofの間に置けるのは「名詞」ですから、名詞の(A) effectivenessが答えになります。

　例題④は、becomeの補語になれるものを選ぶ必要があります。becomeの補語になれるのは「形容詞」であり（形容詞の叙述用法）、このことから形容詞の(B) effectiveが答えになります。

　例題⑤は、同等比較as ... asに現れている語ですが、この語はwas not runningを修飾しています。よって動詞句を修飾していることから、副詞の(C) effectivelyを選ばなければなりません。

　例題⑥は、空所が動詞controlsを修飾していることに気づけば、動詞を修飾する副詞(C) effectivelyが答えになることが分かります。

　このように、品詞がどのような働きをするのかを理解しておくことが、解法のコツです。

（例題解答・訳）
① B（効果的な職場関係を構築することは、どの従業員にとっても極めて重要なスキルです。）
② C（私はその部署は、より効果的に仕事をするためにもっとコミュニケーションが必要だと思います。）
③ A（今や多くの企業がオンライン教育の効果を理解しており、数多くの学習プログラムを用意しています。）
④ B（新しい法律は、来月より施行されます。）
⑤ C（そのシステムは、説明書に記載されているほどには効果的に動いていませんでした。）
⑥ C（前CEOが会社を事実上支配しています。）

Part 5 | Incomplete Sentences

A word or phrase is missing in each of the sentences below. Select the best answer to complete the sentence.

13. Ms. Parson believed both candidates she interviewed were _____ suitable for the position of sales associate.
    (A) equal
    (B) equaled
    (C) equality
    (D) equally
    Ⓐ Ⓑ Ⓒ Ⓓ

14. To accommodate its _____, the popular dry cleaning shop will move next month to 425 S. Hayward Street.
    (A) grow
    (B) growable
    (C) growth
    (D) grown
    Ⓐ Ⓑ Ⓒ Ⓓ

15. Mr. Patel _____ all the machinery at the Winchester Printing Company and turned in his report.
    (A) serviced
    (B) service
    (C) servicing
    (D) to service
    Ⓐ Ⓑ Ⓒ Ⓓ

16. Although the staff spent many weeks preparing for the launch, the consumers responded _____ to the product.
    (A) weak
    (B) weaken
    (C) weakly
    (D) weakness
    Ⓐ Ⓑ Ⓒ Ⓓ

17. Blake, Inc. experienced its third quarter of strong growth owing to its _____ new product line.
    (A) innovate
    (B) innovation
    (C) innovative
    (D) innovator
    Ⓐ Ⓑ Ⓒ Ⓓ

18. Seven years ago, the small retailer started _____ local delivery, which brought an uptick in sales and new customers.
    (A) offer
    (B) offering
    (C) offers
    (D) offered
    Ⓐ Ⓑ Ⓒ Ⓓ

19. Greg has been highly successful in _____ networks with local retail stores while working at the Toronto office.
    (A) develop
    (B) developing
    (C) developed
    (D) development
    Ⓐ Ⓑ Ⓒ Ⓓ

20. The report showed that back pain causes _____ loss for employers due to lower productivity and higher absence rates.
    (A) economic
    (B) economical
    (C) economically
    (D) economy
    Ⓐ Ⓑ Ⓒ Ⓓ

Part 6 Text Completion

Read the text that follows. A word, phrase, or sentence is missing in parts of the text. Select the best answer to complete the text.

Questions 21-24 refer to the following e-mail message.

Hi Fiona,

I wish you good luck with your dinner meeting tomorrow. The Clarkson estate is among our most important clients, and I know they've been considering _____ their business

21.

to one of our rivals. I hope you can convince them to stay with us instead. If you want to really impress them, you could take them to Chez Louis. The owner is a close friend of mine and has agreed to _____ a table for you despite the short notice. There's no

22.

restaurant more highly rated in our part of town, or anywhere else in the city for that matter, and it has a very diverse menu. Normally, you'd have to book at least a month _____ to secure a table there. The Clarkson family likes to feel important, and getting

23.

into Chez Louis on less than a day's notice should certainly accomplish that. You don't have to use the reservation if you have other plans that you think will work out better.

_____.

24.

Best,
Troy Rogers

---

21. (A) move
(B) moved
(C) to move
(D) moving

Ⓐ Ⓑ Ⓒ Ⓓ

22. (A) declare
(B) reserve
(C) clear
(D) launch

Ⓐ Ⓑ Ⓒ Ⓓ

23. (A) in advance
(B) on time
(C) in case
(D) for sure

Ⓐ Ⓑ Ⓒ Ⓓ

24. (A) I just wanted to tell you that I've booked the restaurant you suggested.
(B) Online reservation is now available at almost all of the restaurants in this area.
(C) I just thought I'd give you the option.
(D) You should go to Chez Louis with the Clarkson family.

Ⓐ Ⓑ Ⓒ Ⓓ

Read the following text. Select the best answer for each question.

Questions 25-27 refer to the following advertisement.

NOW OPEN!

ELEGANZA ~ The Ultimate in Fine Dining

You've been hearing all about it in the local news and sharing the anticipation about this latest culinary addition to our local lakeside community. Now, come and experience the ultimate in fine dining at the grand opening of **ELEGANZA**, the elegant Italian restaurant that has just opened its doors for business on the shore of a secluded cove on Lake Ontario.

The Strangiato family, a fixture in our local town of Danforth-Pape for many generations, is now proud to share with fellow residents their love of delectable Mediterranean dishes, exotic foreign traveling and beautiful natural surroundings — all in a single restaurant.

ELEGANZA is open for lunch and dinner daily. We accept online reservations only. Whether you are enjoying an afternoon lunch over the brisk Lake Ontario breezes or dinner on a breathtaking moonlit night, **ELEGANZA** is sure to delight and satisfy.

There is ample parking adjacent to the restaurant. Mention this advertisement to the valet parking staff at the front gate when you drive up, and we will be glad to provide you with priority seating in the restaurant in celebration of our grand opening. The beautiful view is on us.

Welcome, at last, to **ELEGANZA**. Find us at: **www.eleganza-lakeside-dining.com**

25. What is NOT true about Eleganza?

    (A) It has a lakeside dining room.

    (B) It has on-site parking.

    (C) It is open every day.

    (D) It is owned by a multinational corporation.   Ⓐ Ⓑ Ⓒ Ⓓ

26. What type of customer would most likely find the restaurant suitable?

    (A) Businesspeople who prefer to buy boxed lunches

    (B) Couples looking for an urban atmosphere

    (C) Persons seeking a high-priced meal with a view

    (D) Travelers in search of a food court at a shopping mall   Ⓐ Ⓑ Ⓒ Ⓓ

27. What will be offered if a customer mentions the advertisement to the restaurant staff?

    (A) A priority for seats with a nice view

    (B) A free appetizer

    (C) A complimentary meal

    (D) A validated parking ticket   Ⓐ Ⓑ Ⓒ Ⓓ

Travel

Vocabulary

空欄に下から適切な語句を選んで書き入れなさい。なお、動詞については原形で記されています。必要に応じて適切な形に変えなさい。

1. We had to spend time checking in our suitcases and picking them out of the baggage
   (   ).
2. I need to (   ) the meeting with one of my clients for later in the week.
3. The company (   ) the recession and their profit increased dramatically.
4. Because of its (   ), the post office can easily be missed.
5. Technical (   ) on the website made signing up difficult.
6. The market has never worked out as (   ) intended.

> glitches   carousel   originally
> reschedule   shrug off   locale

TOEIC® Listening

Part 1 Photographs

You will hear four short statements. Look at the picture and choose the statement that best describes what you see in the picture.

1.

Ⓐ Ⓑ Ⓒ Ⓓ

2.

Ⓐ Ⓑ Ⓒ Ⓓ

Part **2** Question-Response

You will hear a question or statement and three responses. Listen carefully, and choose the best response to the question or statement.

3. Mark your answer on your answer sheet. Ⓐ   Ⓑ   Ⓒ

4. Mark your answer on your answer sheet. Ⓐ   Ⓑ   Ⓒ

5. Mark your answer on your answer sheet. Ⓐ   Ⓑ   Ⓒ

6. Mark your answer on your answer sheet. Ⓐ   Ⓑ   Ⓒ

Part **3** Conversation

You will hear a short conversation between two or more people. Listen carefully, and select the best response to each question.

7. **Where most likely are the speakers?**
   (A) At an airport
   (B) At a bus terminal
   (C) On a plane
   (D) On a train Ⓐ Ⓑ Ⓒ Ⓓ

8. **Why did the man change his seat?**
   (A) He liked window seats better.
   (B) He wanted to sit next to his child.
   (C) He saw a child who wanted to change her seat.
   (D) He was doing someone a favor. Ⓐ Ⓑ Ⓒ Ⓓ

9. **Who most likely is the woman?**
   (A) A flight attendant
   (B) One of the passengers
   (C) A salesperson
   (D) The mother of a child Ⓐ Ⓑ Ⓒ Ⓓ

You will hear a short talk given by a single speaker. Listen carefully, and select the best response to each question.

10. **Who most likely is the speaker?**
    (A) A travel writer
    (B) A server
    (C) A tour guide
    (D) A wine reviewer
    Ⓐ Ⓑ Ⓒ Ⓓ

11. **What are the listeners asked to do in the processing facility?**
    (A) Keep silent
    (B) Take many pictures
    (C) Taste some wine
    (D) Wear special clothing
    Ⓐ Ⓑ Ⓒ Ⓓ

12. **Where will the listeners go next?**
    (A) To the gift shop
    (B) To the parking lot
    (C) To the processing facility
    (D) To the vineyards
    Ⓐ Ⓑ Ⓒ Ⓓ

Grammar

品詞（その2）

●**品詞の見分け方（その2）**

＜例題＞　次の下線部に当てはまる語句を記号で選びなさい。

(A) decide　　(B) decision　　(C) decisive　　(D) decisively
(E) decided　　(F) deciding

① We need to act quickly and ＿＿＿＿＿＿ to end this strike.
② The economy is regarded as the ＿＿＿＿＿＿ factor for the outcome of this election.
③ I want to try studying before ＿＿＿＿＿＿ on a major.
④ Their irresponsible ＿＿＿＿＿＿ not to attend the conference puzzled everyone.
⑤ The participating firms will be announced once ＿＿＿＿＿＿.
⑥ In recent years, more people have been ＿＿＿＿＿＿ that an MBA course is for them.

　TOEIC® L&Rでは、文の空所に当てはまる適切な品詞を選ぶ問題がよく出題されます。例題をもとに、構造面からどの品詞を空所に入れればよいか考えましょう。

　例題①は、接続詞andにより、副詞quicklyと空所が結ばれて動詞actを修飾していることに気づけば、副詞の (D) decisivelyを選べます。

　例題②は、空所の前に冠詞theが来て、後に名詞factorが来ており、冠詞と名詞の間に入ることができるのは形容詞であることから、(C) decisiveが答えになります。

　例題③は、beforeの後に来ていることがポイントです。形の上では (B) decision と (F) decidingが選べるように思えますが、ここは一種の分詞構文で、節の部分が分詞となり、その前に接続詞beforeが付いた形であることに気づけば、(F) decidingが選べます。before deciding on...はビジネスでよく用いられる言い回しですので、覚えておきましょう（例：Investors need to be reassured before deciding on such investments. 投資家は、そのような投資を決定するには安心を得る必要があります）。名詞decisionを選ぶと、decisionに冠詞theや所有格theirなどが付いていないため、適切ではありません。またこれから決定するという文脈を考えても、動詞decideをもとにした分詞構文を用いるほうがより適切です。

　例題④は、空所の前に形容詞irresponsibleが来ていること、および空所に続くto不定詞が空所にかかることを見抜くことができれば、空所には名詞 (B) decisionが入ることが分かります。

　例題⑤は、onceが接続詞であることを見抜く必要があります。once they (=the participating firms) are decidedの部分がいわゆる分詞構文になり、その結果once decidedになっていることが分かれば、(E) decidedが選べます。例題③のbefore deciding on...と同様、once decidedもビジネスの場面でよく用いられる表現です。

　例題⑥は、現在完了進行形have beenの形が分かれば、(F) decidingを選べます。

　このように、文に絡めた英語の品詞の感覚が習得できれば、品詞の問題は解きやすくなります。

（例題解答・訳）
① D（このストライキを終わらせるために、我々は素早くかつ断固として行動する必要があります。）
② C（経済がこの選挙の決定的要因だとみなされています。）
③ F（私は専攻を決める前に、あらゆることを試してみたいです。）
④ B（会議に出席しないという彼らの責任感の無い決定が、皆を困らせました。）
⑤ E（決定されれば、参加企業が公表されます。）
⑥ F（ここ数年、より多くの人がMBA取得コースはまさに自分たちに適したものだと考えています。）

Part **5** Incomplete Sentences

A word or phrase is missing in each of the sentences below. Select the best answer to complete the sentence.

13. We provide this fitness center for the benefit of all employees; therefore, please follow the rules and use it _____.
    (A) responsibilities   (B) responsibility
    (C) responsible   (D) responsibly   Ⓐ Ⓑ Ⓒ Ⓓ

14. Please contact the site _____ if you have any questions about the registration process or our privacy guidelines.
    (A) administrate   (B) administration
    (C) administrative   (D) administrator   Ⓐ Ⓑ Ⓒ Ⓓ

15. This software allows you to make an _____ slide presentation easily and even add a music track.
    (A) animate   (B) animated
    (C) animatedly   (D) animation   Ⓐ Ⓑ Ⓒ Ⓓ

16. The local government plans to improve roads that _____ suburbs with major commuting routes into the city.
    (A) connect   (B) connectable
    (C) connecting   (D) connection   Ⓐ Ⓑ Ⓒ Ⓓ

17. The manager worked well into the night on the project and was _____ to realize he was not at all sleepy.
    (A) surprise   (B) surprised
    (C) surprising   (D) surprisingly   Ⓐ Ⓑ Ⓒ Ⓓ

18. Our records indicate that you have the Galaxy Banquet Hall _____ for Friday, April 22.
    (A) reserve   (B) reservations
    (C) reserved   (D) reserving   Ⓐ Ⓑ Ⓒ Ⓓ

19. After _____ to become independent and trying to develop his own company, Bud McCloskey faces hardships that might cause him to throw away the idea.
    (A) decide   (B) decision
    (C) decided   (D) deciding   Ⓐ Ⓑ Ⓒ Ⓓ

20. The glitches in the computer program were appearing with increasing _____ until Ms. Cornell finally called the IT staff for help.
    (A) regular   (B) regularity
    (C) regularly   (D) regulate   Ⓐ Ⓑ Ⓒ Ⓓ

Part **6** Text Completion

Read the text that follows. A word, phrase, or sentence is missing in parts of the text. Select the best answer to complete the text.

Questions 21-24 refer to the following article.

How to Combat Jet Lag

Traveling the world is exciting. The jet lag that comes with it, however, is not. Although traversing numerous time zones to get to an exotic locale is unavoidable, the sleepiness and disorientation that comes with it can be _____. And who would know better than
21.
someone who _____ jet lag regularly for work? Richard Kleck, a cabin crew member
22.
on the United Arab Emirates' A380 fleet, shares his advice with us:

Drink plenty of water during the flight to combat jet lag. The best advice is to go back to basics — appreciate your body and _____ healthy. If your body's telling you to sleep,
23.
you should make sure you get lots of it.

Once you get home, you should get a good night's sleep of at least eight hours. This helps you refresh and readjust. _____. But it's important to try and get back to your routine,
24.
whatever that may be, as soon as possible. Once a sense of normalcy sets in, shrugging off that jet lag becomes so much easier.

---

21. (A) less
(B) lessen
(C) lessened
(D) lesser

Ⓐ Ⓑ Ⓒ Ⓓ

22. (A) comes to
(B) deals with
(C) puts off
(D) hits upon

Ⓐ Ⓑ Ⓒ Ⓓ

23. (A) stay
(B) do
(C) leave
(D) have

Ⓐ Ⓑ Ⓒ Ⓓ

24. (A) Sleeping works well if you want to get away from your daily concerns.
(B) Keeping awake is the best way to conquer jet lag.
(C) Please try not to eat a lot before you go to sleep.
(D) Let your body dictate your pace.

Ⓐ Ⓑ Ⓒ Ⓓ

Part 7 Single Passage

Read the following text. Select the best answer for each question.

Questions 25-27 refer to the following text message chain.

> **Gabriele Vost (3:43 P.M.)**
> Hey, Pat. Would you happen to have the flight times for our upcoming trip to Germany handy? I must have deleted the e-mail by mistake.

> **Patrick Heintz (3:47 P.M.)**
> Yep! Will forward the itinerary to you now. Have you finished working on our presentation for the University of Kassel?

> **Gabriele Vost (3:52 P.M.)**
> Thanks. Yes, am putting the finishing touches on the presentation as we speak. Should be a great event. Lots of heavy hitters in the petroglyph industry will be there. Any free time to go over it before we leave?

> **Patrick Heintz (3:55 P.M.)**
> No can do. I'm booked up solid for the next few days. Can you ask Jan to do it?

> **Patrick Heintz (3:57 P.M.)**
> Wait, I'll change that other appointment I have... OK, I can spare a couple of hours on Monday afternoon. Will that work for you?

> **Gabriele Vost (4:02 P.M.)**
> Perfect. I'm free from 3:00 Monday. Meet at that new café around the corner from the office. Have a good weekend!

25. Why does Ms. Vost text Mr. Heintz?

    (A) To go out on a date

    (B) To send an itinerary

    (C) To complete the draft together

    (D) To check the departure time of the flight   Ⓐ Ⓑ Ⓒ Ⓓ

26. Why are Mr. Heintz and Ms. Vost traveling to Germany?

    (A) To organize a tour

    (B) To do sightseeing

    (C) To give a presentation

    (D) To start a new business   Ⓐ Ⓑ Ⓒ Ⓓ

27. At 3:57 P.M., what does Mr. Heintz mean when he writes, "Will that work for you"?

    (A) He wonders if Ms. Vost will have the document ready by Monday.

    (B) He wonders if Ms. Vost has a job interview on Monday.

    (C) He wonders if Ms. Vost has time to meet on Monday.

    (D) He wonders if Ms. Vost will be taking a day off on Monday.

    Ⓐ Ⓑ Ⓒ Ⓓ

Warm-up

Vocabulary

空欄に下から適切な語を選んで書き入れなさい。なお、動詞については原形で記されています。必要に応じて適切な形に変えなさい。

1. I'm so (　　　　　) to hear that you are coming to the party.
2. The (　　　　　) stand sells the usual selection of sugary snacks.
3. I (　　　　　) her way of facing difficulty without making any complaints.
4. He told me of his future plan to (　　　　　) it as an actor.
5. Her lips (　　　　　) and tears rolled down her cheeks.
6. We couldn't afford to stay at the (　　　　　) hotel that the travel agency had recommended to us.

luxurious	concession	quiver
make	thrilled	admire

TOEIC® Listening

Part **1** Photographs 🎧10

You will hear four short statements. Look at the picture and choose the statement that best describes what you see in the picture.

1.

Ⓐ Ⓑ Ⓒ Ⓓ

2.

Ⓐ Ⓑ Ⓒ Ⓓ

Part 2 Question-Response

You will hear a question or statement and three responses. Listen carefully, and choose the best response to the question or statement.

3. Mark your answer on your answer sheet.   Ⓐ Ⓑ Ⓒ

4. Mark your answer on your answer sheet.   Ⓐ Ⓑ Ⓒ

5. Mark your answer on your answer sheet.   Ⓐ Ⓑ Ⓒ

6. Mark your answer on your answer sheet.   Ⓐ Ⓑ Ⓒ

Part 3 Conversation

You will hear a short conversation between two or more people. Listen carefully, and select the best response to each question.

7. **What will the man do next week?**
   (A) Go to a Rockets game
   (B) Go to see his son's game
   (C) Go to see his daughter's play
   (D) Go to see Harrison Loman playing   Ⓐ Ⓑ Ⓒ Ⓓ

8. **What does the man imply when he says, "We can't miss that"?**
   (A) His child's performance is important.
   (B) His parents are coming to visit.
   (C) His daughter wants to do something else.
   (D) His wife cannot miss the game.   Ⓐ Ⓑ Ⓒ Ⓓ

9. **What does the woman say about her son?**
   (A) He has a game on that day.
   (B) He may not want to attend.
   (C) He will ask his friend to go.
   (D) He will be excited.   Ⓐ Ⓑ Ⓒ Ⓓ

You will hear a short talk given by a single speaker. Listen carefully, and select the best response to each question.

10. **According to the advertisement, what is unique about TriStar Cinemas?**

    (A) Its food

    (B) Its prices

    (C) Its seats

    (D) Its size   Ⓐ   Ⓑ   Ⓒ   Ⓓ

11. **How many places can a visitor buy food and drinks at TriStar Cinemas?**

    (A) 1

    (B) 2

    (C) 3

    (D) 4   Ⓐ   Ⓑ   Ⓒ   Ⓓ

12. **What are listeners encouraged to do online?**

    (A) Check the movie schedule

    (B) Find directions to the theater

    (C) Leave a review of the cinemas

    (D) Register for a member's card   Ⓐ   Ⓑ   Ⓒ   Ⓓ

Grammar

時　制

1. 過去形と現在完了形

＜例文＞　（ⅰ）Did you see the Turkish art exhibition?
　　　　　（ⅱ）Have you seen the Turkish art exhibition?
　　　　　（あなたはトルコ美術の展覧会を見ましたか。）

　動詞の過去形と現在完了形はどちらも過去にあった出来事を指して言う言い方ですが、微妙なニュアンスの差が出ることもあります。例えばトルコ美術の展覧会を見たかを尋ねている上の例文の場合、例文（ⅰ）は展覧会は現在行われておらず、ここで展覧会が行われていたときに見たかどうか尋ねるのに用いられ、例文（ⅱ）は展覧会の開催中で、もう展覧会を見に行ったかどうかを尋ねており、それについて意見を聞きたい時などに好んで使われる場合があります。
　次のような文でも、過去形と現在完了形のニュアンスの差が現れています。

＜例文＞　（ⅲ）My father lived here all his life.
　　　　　（ⅳ）My father has lived here all his life.
　　　　　（私の父は生涯、ここで暮らしていました。）

　例文（ⅲ）では、亡くなった父を回顧して述べている時などに用いられるのに対し、例文（ⅳ）は父が存命で、今もまだここに住み続けていることを述べる時に使うのに適しています。
　このように、現在完了形は「現在との関わり」が示唆されているため、justなど今行ったばかりであることを強調する副詞や、already, yetなど既に行ったことを明確に示す副詞と結びつきやすいと言えます（The plane has just landed. / I've already told her about the meeting.）。

2. 過去形と過去完了形

＜例文＞　（ⅴ）When I arrived at the bus stop, the bus left.
　　　　　（私がバス停に着くと、バスが出発しました。）
　　　　　（ⅵ）When I arrived at the bus stop, the bus had already left.
　　　　　（私がバス停に着くと、バスは既に出発していました。）

　例文（ⅴ）は従属節の動詞arrivedと主節の動詞leftがどちらも過去形であることから、ほぼ同時に出来事が起こったことを示しています。一方、例文（ⅵ）は、主節に過去完了形が使われていることから、その行為が既に行われていたことを強調しています。つまり、バス停に着いた時には、すでにバスが出発していたことを明確に示しています。このように、過去完了形は、過去にあった出来事の時間差をはっきり示したい時に用いられます。
　このことから、過去の事柄を振り返って述べる時に、その出来事の順序をはっきりさせる必要がない場合には、例文（ⅶ）のように、すべて過去形を用いて言います。

＜例文＞　（ⅶ）I worked in elementary schools for 35 years and retired in 2022.
　　　　　（私は小学校に35年間勤め、2022年に定年退職しました。）

TOEIC® Reading

Part **5** Incomplete Sentences

A word or phrase is missing in each of the sentences below. Select the best answer to complete the sentence.

13. As part of our new campaign starting next week, we _____ customers an additional discount for ordering two or more items.
    (A) had offered   (B) offer
    (C) to offer   (D) will offer   Ⓐ Ⓑ Ⓒ Ⓓ

14. Unfortunately, we are completely booked on the night you _____; however, we have rooms on the following night if you are interested.
    (A) requested   (B) are requested
    (C) request   (D) requesting   Ⓐ Ⓑ Ⓒ Ⓓ

15. Fast fashion is a term used to describe the problem of buying too much clothing which cannot be recycled or _____ second-hand.
    (A) have sold   (B) sell
    (C) selling   (D) sold   Ⓐ Ⓑ Ⓒ Ⓓ

16. More and more companies are removing their names from their logos _____ them easier to identify on smartphones.
    (A) had made   (B) has made
    (C) to make   (D) will make   Ⓐ Ⓑ Ⓒ Ⓓ

17. The initial estimate _____ to anticipate the rising cost of fuel; thus, the project went over budget by a large margin.
    (A) failed   (B) fails
    (C) is failing   (D) will fail   Ⓐ Ⓑ Ⓒ Ⓓ

18. To ease traffic, the Haven City Council _____ a new measure limiting the number of delivery vehicles on downtown streets during the day.
    (A) had passed   (B) is passed
    (C) passed   (D) passing   Ⓐ Ⓑ Ⓒ Ⓓ

19. Ms. Britt included colorful charts and graphs in her presentation _____ that her points were clearly understood and memorable.
    (A) to ensure   (B) will ensure
    (C) is ensuring   (D) ensures   Ⓐ Ⓑ Ⓒ Ⓓ

20. Amelia must be irritated at the denial notice about her proposal; her lips quivered as if she was about _____.
    (A) cry   (B) to cry
    (C) crying   (D) cried   Ⓐ Ⓑ Ⓒ Ⓓ

Part 6 Text Completion

Read the text that follows. A word, phrase, or sentence is missing in parts of the text. Select the best answer to complete the text.

Questions 21-24 refer to the following invitation.

Invitation to Special Event for City Museum Members

Members of the Ravensbrück City Museum are invited to _____ talk on the eve of the
                                                                           21.
public opening of our new Renaissance art exhibit, which starts on July 18. _____.
                                                                                    22.
She holds a Ph.D. in art history from the University of Berlin and is currently a
professor at the university. She _____ about the events leading up to the Renaissance
                                         23.
cultural boom and how the art pieces in the exhibit fit into those historical events. Please
join us on July 17 at 7:00 p.m. Light refreshments will _____ the talk. RSVP at:
                                                                24.
www.ravensbrueck-city-museum.org/events

---

21. (A) an informative
   (B) a familiar
   (C) a putative
   (D) a quantitative

   (A) (B) (C) (D)

22. (A) The museum curator encourages the public to join the museum at any level of sponsorship.
   (B) Dr. Angelica Krüger, the country's foremost expert on Renaissance painting and history, is the main guest of the event.
   (C) The Renaissance exhibit is sponsored by the Art Research Institute and by a grant from the city.
   (D) Your membership entitles you to talks like this and other perks, such as free parking and audio tours.

   (A) (B) (C) (D)

23. (A) has spoken
   (B) speaks
   (C) spoke
   (D) will speak

   (A) (B) (C) (D)

24. (A) continue
   (B) follow
   (C) occur
   (D) provide

   (A) (B) (C) (D)

Part **7** Single Passage

Read the following text. Select the best answer for each question.

Questions 25-27 refer to the following news article.

Exploring the World of Art Through High Digital Technology

A popular art museum in the city is using Robotic Process Automation, a cutting-edge form of artificial intelligence, to attract customers, enhance exhibitions, and break down physical and language barriers.

Even if the facility's new robot does kind of freak out the visitors at first.

Nowhere was that more on display than at the Modern Museum of Arts and Sciences in downtown Philadelphia recently. There, a group of tourists from overseas countries chatted in different languages with a walking, talking humanoid named "Jupiter."

Later, the five-foot-tall robot led a group of local schoolchildren on a guided tour of the museum. The kids said they enjoyed the experience, but admitted it felt "kinda freaky" at first talking to a machine.

The museum, located in Philadelphia's Queen Village neighborhood at the plaza off Catharine Street near Front Street, has seen visitor rates skyrocket since Jupiter arrived last month.

And for those who cannot visit the museum in person, Jupiter is also fitted with an internal camera and speaker, allowing remote viewers to marvel at artworks, converse with museum staff in Zoom sessions and convey their feelings through hand and facial gestures — all from the comfort of their own home.

Karen Cho, director of the Philadelphia Arts Commission, said: "One participant told me, 'I felt like I'd left my disabled body behind, allowing my senses to roam free.' Jupiter has even helped push around persons in wheelchairs. Everybody loves this robot."

25. What is NOT true about Jupiter?

    (A) It is used in remote tours.

    (B) It has a human figure.

    (C) It helps remote visitors talk to museum employees.

    (D) It works full time in the museum gift shop.   Ⓐ Ⓑ Ⓒ Ⓓ

26. Who is Ms. Cho?

    (A) She is a teacher of museology.

    (B) She is head of the city's arts commission.

    (C) She is the researcher who developed Jupiter.

    (D) She is a remote-viewing participant.   Ⓐ Ⓑ Ⓒ Ⓓ

27. What is indicated about the museum?

    (A) It displays lots of famous artworks.

    (B) It built a new elevator for disabled people.

    (C) It created a mascot character.

    (D) It makes use of new AI technology.   Ⓐ Ⓑ Ⓒ Ⓓ

Meetings

Warm-up

Vocabulary

空欄に下から適切な語句を選んで書き入れなさい。なお、動詞については原形で記されています。必要に応じて適切な形に変えなさい。

1. We must make a budget plan for the next (　　　　) year.
2. The NPO group (　　　　) food and medicine to the disaster victims.
3. I had some (　　　　) business come up, so I must leave now.
4. On (　　　　) thought, I shouldn't take the company's head-hunting offer.
5. With the rapid development of online meetings, it's time for us to consider having an online employee (　　　　).
6. You should (　　　　) your report for grammar and spelling before you turn it in.

> distribute　　　　fiscal　　　　go over
> orientation　　　urgent　　　second

TOEIC® Listening

Part **1** Photographs 🎧14

You will hear four short statements. Look at the picture and choose the statement that best describes what you see in the picture.

1.

Ⓐ　Ⓑ　Ⓒ　Ⓓ

2.

Ⓐ　Ⓑ　Ⓒ　Ⓓ

Part **2** Question-Response

You will hear a question or statement and three responses. Listen carefully, and choose the best response to the question or statement.

3. Mark your answer on your answer sheet.   (A) (B) (C)

4. Mark your answer on your answer sheet.   (A) (B) (C)

5. Mark your answer on your answer sheet.   (A) (B) (C)

6. Mark your answer on your answer sheet.   (A) (B) (C)

Part **3** Conversation

You will hear a short conversation between two or more people. Listen carefully, and select the best response to each question.

7. **What will the speakers discuss at their meeting?**
   (A) Conference duties
   (B) New staff training
   (C) Product advertising
   (D) Product development   (A) (B) (C) (D)

8. **Who will join the meeting?**
   (A) A consumer focus group
   (B) Managers of other offices
   (C) All the branch staff members
   (D) Some new clients   (A) (B) (C) (D)

9. **What does the man mean when he says, "let me move a few things around"?**
   (A) He will change his schedule.
   (B) He will move to a new office.
   (C) He will join the meeting remotely.
   (D) He will send the other managers his ideas.   (A) (B) (C) (D)

You will hear a short talk given by a single speaker. Listen carefully, and select the best response to each question.

Employee Orientation Schedule	
9:00	Greetings from President George Essex
9:30	Talk by Personnel Department Director, Dr. Lucille Blakemon
10:30	Tour of office with Roger Jenkins
12:00	Lunch with selected department heads

10. **Why is the speaker asking for the listeners' help?**

    (A) His previous assistant is unavailable.

    (B) His supervisor asked him to get help.

    (C) He forgot about the orientation.

    (D) He has to go out of town on business.   Ⓐ Ⓑ Ⓒ Ⓓ

11. **How many listeners does the speaker need help from?**

    (A) 1

    (B) 2

    (C) 3

    (D) 4   Ⓐ Ⓑ Ⓒ Ⓓ

12. **Look at the graphic. Who most likely is the speaker?**

    (A) Calvin Roberts

    (B) Lucille Blakemon

    (C) George Essex

    (D) Roger Jenkins   Ⓐ Ⓑ Ⓒ Ⓓ

Grammar

動　詞

1. 自動詞と他動詞

　TOEIC® L&Rの問題では適切な動詞を選ぶ問題があります。文から適切な意味を探り出すことも必要ですが、自動詞と他動詞の違いから適切な動詞を選ぶ問題も出ます。次の例文で、自動詞と他動詞の違いを確認しましょう。

＜例文＞　（ⅰ）a.　The plane rose above the clouds.（その飛行機は雲の上に出ました。）
　　　　　　　b.　He raised the window awnings.（彼は窓の日よけを上げました。）

　　　　　（ⅱ）a.　A cat lay still in front of the gate.（猫が門の前に静かにたたずんでいました。）
　　　　　　　b.　Mourners laid flowers at a memorial site.
　　　　　　　（哀悼者が記念の場所に花を手向けました。）

　　　　　（ⅲ）a.　A postman arrived with a parcel for me.
　　　　　　　（郵便局員が私あての小包を持って到着しました。）
　　　　　　　b.　The climbers finally reached the summit of the mountain.
　　　　　　　（登山者たちはようやく山の頂上に辿り着きました。）

　例文（ⅰ），（ⅱ），（ⅲ）で使われている動詞はa, bどちらもよく似た意味ですが、**aが自動詞**で、**bが他動詞**です。他動詞の場合は後に目的語を取ることから判別できます。例文（ⅱ）a では、自動詞lieの過去形layは、他動詞layの原形と同じ形になりますので、注意が必要です。

2. 受動態

　自動詞は目的語を伴わないため、受動態の形では用いられません。

＜例文＞　（ⅳ）× Something terrible was happened to me.
　　　　　　　○ Something terrible happened to me.（ひどいことが私に起こりました。）

　目的語を伴う他動詞であっても、受動態にできない場合があります。受動態は動作動詞（action verb）を用いて、動詞の行動が目的語に影響を及ぼしていることを明確に示しています。このことから、例文（ⅴ）〜（ⅶ）のような「状態（state）」を表す動詞（＝状態動詞）は、受動態にできません。

＜例文＞　（ⅴ）× His father is resembled by James. / × James is resembled by his father.
　　　　　　　○ James resembles his father.（ジェームズは彼の父親に似ています。）

　　　　　（ⅵ）× At least $1,000 will be cost by the trip.
　　　　　　　○ The trip will cost you at least $1,000.（その旅行には少なくとも1千ドルかかります。）

　　　　　（ⅶ）× You are suited by the blue jacket.
　　　　　　　○ The blue jacket suits you.（その青いジャケットはあなたに合っています。）

Part 5 Incomplete Sentences

A word or phrase is missing in each of the sentences below. Select the best answer to complete the sentence.

13. The new sales division chief has promised to _____ an international presence for the company's popular products.
    (A) acknowledge
    (B) establish
    (C) request
    (D) spread
    Ⓐ Ⓑ Ⓒ Ⓓ

14. Sam Rich, who headed Sam's Productions as CEO and co-owner, announced that his company would _____ its R&D division with that of Lennox Picture Films.
    (A) merge
    (B) disturb
    (C) emerge
    (D) collect
    Ⓐ Ⓑ Ⓒ Ⓓ

15. During the meeting, Mr. Kim's assistant _____ standing at the back of the room.
    (A) sent
    (B) left
    (C) remained
    (D) waited
    Ⓐ Ⓑ Ⓒ Ⓓ

16. The company wants to _____ any more shutdowns that would keep it from recovering its lost production output.
    (A) agree
    (B) avoid
    (C) contact
    (D) pursue
    Ⓐ Ⓑ Ⓒ Ⓓ

17. The regional government published plastic-recycling guidelines that aim to _____ plastic waste by 30 percent.
    (A) complete
    (B) dispose
    (C) enforce
    (D) reduce
    Ⓐ Ⓑ Ⓒ Ⓓ

18. The city council announced that eight percent of the budget of the next fiscal year would be _____ for disaster relief.
    (A) funded
    (B) passed
    (C) allocated
    (D) placed
    Ⓐ Ⓑ Ⓒ Ⓓ

19. Andrew has _____ to a position of great responsibility after his excellent work on the three-year-long research project.
    (A) pulled
    (B) promoted
    (C) raised
    (D) risen
    Ⓐ Ⓑ Ⓒ Ⓓ

20. The members of Bei-Wei Fitness Club have been _____ that there will be a small increase in the fee.
    (A) notified
    (B) known
    (C) discussed
    (D) contacted
    Ⓐ Ⓑ Ⓒ Ⓓ

Part **6** Text Completion

Read the text that follows. A word, phrase, or sentence is missing in parts of the text. Select the best answer to complete the text.

Questions 21-24 refer to the following memorandum.

TO: Alex Dudden
FROM: Elisa Sullivan
DATE: 14 December 2023
SUBJECT: Status of Thomas Ward

Thomas Ward initiated a meeting with our company's Human Resources Department manager to discuss the status of his employment as he considers taking an extended leave of absence from the company, which _____ in 2022. He is emphatic that his family
                                        21.
situation makes it problematic, if not outright impossible, for him to return at this time to his _____ as a full-time researcher in the Silicon Chip Development Department.
       22.
_____ . Please contact Mr. Ward to discuss the details of any such projects. We _____
  23.   **24.**
that after the new year we would meet again to negotiate his future engagement with the company.

---

21. (A) began
   (B) begin
   (C) beginning
   (D) begins

        Ⓐ   Ⓑ   Ⓒ   Ⓓ

23. (A) However, he is eager to work at home on any short-term projects the company may have.
   (B) It goes without saying that the content of the meeting should be kept confidential.
   (C) Hence, he is well prepared to get back to the workplace.
   (D) We have discussed the possibility of promoting him to manager of our overseas branch.

        Ⓐ   Ⓑ   Ⓒ   Ⓓ

22. (A) salary
   (B) benefit
   (C) position
   (D) task

        Ⓐ   Ⓑ   Ⓒ   Ⓓ

24. (A) agreed
   (B) recalled
   (C) observed
   (D) objected

        Ⓐ   Ⓑ   Ⓒ   Ⓓ

Part 7 Single Passage

Read the following text. Select the best answer for each question.

Questions 25-28 refer to the following online discussion.

PLANNING DEPT. TEAM MEETING • members online: 23

Juan Hinojosa Kitazawa   9:02 AM
Good morning, team.
Is everybody here? Let's go over today's agenda. Top of the list is the conflict over the scheduling of conference halls here at the Convention Center. This has been causing us complications. Julie, how about a rundown of where things stand?

Julie Boyle   9:06 AM
Good morning.
Yes, here is the latest: We recently scheduled the Global Documentary Film Festival for October 23 in Hall 1. The problem is we already had reserved that space for the Children's Memorial Fund Annual Meeting. That's set in stone and cannot be changed. But the film festival is now threatening to cancel their event and sue us if they cannot have Hall 1, our biggest space, as we had promised them.

Juan Hinojosa Kitazawa   9:12 AM
This is a very serious matter.
Who is directly responsible for this major mix-up?

Anton Belovsky   9:14 AM
That would be me, Mr. K. Please allow me to explain. It was an oversight on the part of my section. We deeply apologize. Today, our representative is proceeding with negotiations with both parties. We're hopeful of a positive outcome.

Julie Boyle   9:17 AM
That's good news. Let's keep our fingers crossed.
One idea: How about leasing to the film festival Hall 19 — plus the adjacent Hall 20 at no extra cost? We have both these halls open for the next few months.

Juan Hinojosa Kitazawa   9:20 AM
Brilliant idea, Julie!
Run it past the legal and accounting departments as well to get their take on it. Anton?

Anton Belovsky   9:22 AM
I hadn't thought about offering the two other halls, but it might just work. Let me consult my section about it. The negotiator is just getting ready to leave and meet with the two sides. I'll brief her immediately too.

Juan Hinojosa Kitazawa   9:25 AM
Fine. Julie and Anton, I want a full report about this matter on my desk first thing tomorrow morning. I'll be expecting it.
Any other business to take care of, anybody? If not, meeting adjourned.

25. **What is Mr. Kitazawa discussing with Ms. Boyle and Mr. Belovsky?**

    (A) The budget for the next fiscal year

    (B) A scheduling issue that has caused big problems

    (C) Watching a movie at a film festival

    (D) Donating to a memorial fund for children   Ⓐ Ⓑ Ⓒ Ⓓ

26. **What did Mr. Belovsky mistakenly do?**

    (A) He forgot to attend an upcoming event at the convention center.

    (B) He double-booked the convention center's biggest hall.

    (C) He canceled a customer's event.

    (D) He neglected to clean up the hall before leasing it.   Ⓐ Ⓑ Ⓒ Ⓓ

27. **What is indicated about the two alternative conference halls?**

    (A) They will not be big enough for the film festival.

    (B) One of them is under renovation.

    (C) One would be paid for and the other one would be used for free.

    (D) None of them is available now.   Ⓐ Ⓑ Ⓒ Ⓓ

28. **What does Mr. Kitazawa want the other two staff members to do the next day?**

    (A) Give an oral presentation to the two clients

    (B) Have the legal department file a lawsuit against the clients

    (C) Make a detailed written report and leave it at his office

    (D) Ignore the problem as a way to smooth things over   Ⓐ Ⓑ Ⓒ Ⓓ

Warm-up

Vocabulary

　空欄に下から適切な語を選んで書き入れなさい。なお、動詞については原形で記されています。必要に応じて適切な形に変えなさい。

1.　The (　　　　　) line in our manufacturing division is still going strong to this day.

2.　These days more and more businesses have been considering (　　　　　) their branch offices abroad.

3.　Computer failures caused (　　　　　) at the airport.

4.　The new tax plan will put a lot of small (　　　　　) out of business.

5.　He is a great (　　　　　) to this team, and we'd love to have him stick around.

6.　According to our (　　　　　), we are still 200,000 yen short.

relocate	addition	firms
calculations	assembly	delays

TOEIC® Listening

Part **1** Photographs 🎧18

You will hear four short statements. Look at the picture and choose the statement that best describes what you see in the picture.

1.

Ⓐ　Ⓑ　Ⓒ　Ⓓ

2.

Ⓐ　Ⓑ　Ⓒ　Ⓓ

Part 2 Question-Response

You will hear a question or statement and three responses. Listen carefully, and choose the best response to the question or statement.

3. Mark your answer on your answer sheet.   Ⓐ   Ⓑ   Ⓒ

4. Mark your answer on your answer sheet.   Ⓐ   Ⓑ   Ⓒ

5. Mark your answer on your answer sheet.   Ⓐ   Ⓑ   Ⓒ

6. Mark your answer on your answer sheet.   Ⓐ   Ⓑ   Ⓒ

Part 3 Conversation

You will hear a short conversation between two or more people. Listen carefully, and select the best response to each question.

7. **Who most likely is the man?**
    (A) An inspector
    (B) A job candidate
    (C) A new employee
    (D) A supervisor   Ⓐ   Ⓑ   Ⓒ   Ⓓ

8. **What is mentioned about the helmet?**
    (A) It is very large.
    (B) It is found in the warehouse.
    (C) It is hard to replace.
    (D) It is a requirement.   Ⓐ   Ⓑ   Ⓒ   Ⓓ

9. **What will the man do next?**
    (A) Fill out more paperwork
    (B) Learn to drive a vehicle
    (C) Start repairs on an airplane
    (D) Watch a safety video   Ⓐ   Ⓑ   Ⓒ   Ⓓ

Part **4** Talk

You will hear a short talk given by a single speaker. Listen carefully, and select the best response to each question.

10. **What is the purpose of the call?**

    (A) To inquire about construction work

    (B) To offer an attractive job

    (C) To offer a permanent job

    (D) To schedule a job interview   

11. **What could the listener do in the future?**

    (A) Continue at the speaker's firm

    (B) Get a stable position at a branch office

    (C) Receive a positive review by the speaker

    (D) Register at a temporary employment agency   Ⓐ Ⓑ Ⓒ Ⓓ

12. **What does the speaker ask the listener to do next?**

    (A) Wait for the company's reply

    (B) Send an e-mail message

    (C) Meet the receptionist

    (D) Call her office   Ⓐ Ⓑ Ⓒ Ⓓ

Grammar

名詞

●名詞の様々な使い方

　TOEIC® L&Rでは、空欄の語彙を選択する問題の一つとして、名詞を題材にしたものがあります。文から適切な名詞を探り出す必要がありますが、名詞の使い方を知っておくことも、名詞選択の決め手になります。

　以下の様々な使い方から、名詞を用いた表現を理解しましょう。

<例文> （ⅰ）You can see lots of historical architecture and enjoy hot springs. I believe that Budapest is <u>worth the visit</u>.

（歴史的建造物をたくさん見られるし、温泉も楽しめるので、ブダペストは行くべきところですよ。）

（ⅱ）A ticket for the musical costs 20,000 yen, but you'll think it was <u>worth the expense</u> after seeing the performance.

（そのミュージカルのチケットは2万円するのですが、きっと演技を見た後は、支出に見合うものだったと思うと思います。）

（ⅲ）I'm sorry I can't be <u>of any help</u>.

（何もお役に立つことができず申し訳ありません。）

（ⅳ）I didn't do it <u>on purpose</u>. It was an accident.

（わざとそれをやったのではありません。偶然だったのです。）

（ⅴ）He won the 800-meter race <u>with ease</u>.

（彼は800mレースで難なく勝ちました。）

（ⅵ）She worked as <u>a sales representative</u> for several companies, including an automobile business and an insurance company.

（彼女は販売員として自動車会社や保険会社などいくつかの会社で働きました。）

　例文（ⅰ）、（ⅱ）では、worthの後に名詞を置いて「〜する価値がある」の意味を示しています。Budapest is worth visiting. のように動名詞を用いることもできます。ここに挙げた例以外にも、worth the effort（努力するに値する）など、様々な使い方ができます。

　例文（ⅲ）、（ⅳ）、（ⅴ）は、前置詞の後に抽象名詞を用いた形です。例文（ⅲ）では「of＋抽象名詞」で形容詞的な意味になることから、of helpでhelpfulの意味になります。Can I be of any assistance?（何か私でお役に立てることがありますか）などもビジネスの場面でよく使われます。例文（ⅳ）on purpose「わざと」、例文（ⅴ）with ease「簡単に、難なく」のように、前置詞と抽象名詞で様々な意味になることを覚えておきましょう。

　例文（ⅵ）のa sales representativeは複数の語から作られた複合語で、TOEIC® L&Rでは他にもhuman resources（人材、人事部）、warehouse（倉庫）、board members（役員）、boardroom（会議室）など、ビジネスに関する複合語がたくさん出てきます。TOEIC® L&Rの問題演習を通して、これらのビジネス関連の複合語も身につけましょう。

TOEIC® Reading

Part **5** Incomplete Sentences

A word or phrase is missing in each of the sentences below. Select the best answer to complete the sentence.

13. A recent _____ published in a medical journal reveals that people who work past the age of 65 usually live longer than those who do not.
    (A) education
    (B) exam
    (C) learning
    (D) study
    Ⓐ Ⓑ Ⓒ Ⓓ

14. The manufacturer announced Monday its intention to get _____ from the government to resume production as soon as possible.
    (A) approval
    (B) progress
    (C) protocol
    (D) restriction
    Ⓐ Ⓑ Ⓒ Ⓓ

15. Though our company agrees with the measure in _____, we have some reservations about how it will be carried out.
    (A) conclusion
    (B) format
    (C) illusion
    (D) principle
    Ⓐ Ⓑ Ⓒ Ⓓ

16. If you notice any _____ in the report data, please let the sales team know right away.
    (A) declarations
    (B) deliberations
    (C) disapprovals
    (D) discrepancies
    Ⓐ Ⓑ Ⓒ Ⓓ

17. The personnel department is planning to interview six _____ for the associate sales position between March 3 and March 10.
    (A) candidates
    (B) executives
    (C) opposites
    (D) researchers
    Ⓐ Ⓑ Ⓒ Ⓓ

18. The new machinery increased the _____ of Housman Inc.'s Rockridge manufacturing plant by 25 percent.
    (A) service
    (B) foundation
    (C) store
    (D) efficiency
    Ⓐ Ⓑ Ⓒ Ⓓ

19. The bank _____ at the end of the year will tell us fairly accurately how we have been doing.
    (A) account
    (B) balance
    (C) check
    (D) order
    Ⓐ Ⓑ Ⓒ Ⓓ

20. The presentation about our newly developed computers was ruined by his poor _____.
    (A) delivery
    (B) announcement
    (C) transmission
    (D) publication
    Ⓐ Ⓑ Ⓒ Ⓓ

Read the text that follows. A word, phrase, or sentence is missing in parts of the text. Select the best answer to complete the text.

Questions 21-24 refer to the following advertisement.

Assistant Store Managers Wanted

The grocery chain All Organic Foods (AOF) plans to _____ its newest location in Las
                    21.

Vegas, Nevada, on April 23. _____, we are currently looking for dynamic, reliable and
          22.

personable individuals to work as assistant managers at our new store.

Primary _____ include hiring and training staff, maintaining store inventory, resolving
     23.

customer complaints and assisting in the everyday operation of the new AOF store, which will be fully unionized.

Applicants must have three or more years of experience in the retail grocery industry.
_____. Applications are available on our website at **www.all-organic-foods.com/jobs**
 24.

---

21. (A) expand
 (B) open
 (C) relocate
 (D) occupy
     Ⓐ Ⓑ Ⓒ Ⓓ

22. (A) Consequently
 (B) However
 (C) Afterwards
 (D) Otherwise
     Ⓐ Ⓑ Ⓒ Ⓓ

23. (A) subscriptions
 (B) descriptions
 (C) appointments
 (D) responsibilities
     Ⓐ Ⓑ Ⓒ Ⓓ

24. (A) Interested applicants without any retail experience can apply for this job.
 (B) Tech-savvy youths are the best candidates for this position.
 (C) We are very happy to work with you at this newly opened supermarket soon.
 (D) Outstanding communication and customer service skills are required.
     Ⓐ Ⓑ Ⓒ Ⓓ

Part 7 Single Passage

Read the following text. Select the best answer for each question.

Questions 25-28 refer to the following newsletter article.

At Diligence Logistics, we celebrate change. Firstly, we are grateful to Sheila Robertson, who has been on the Human Resources team for eight years. Sheila started out as a section chief and quickly demonstrated her impressive knowledge and expertise in handling employee affairs. – [1] –. She rose to Human Resources Manager at the beginning of last year. Sheila will be missed dearly by everyone, especially the HR team. The managerial position will be taken over by Mr. Jackson Rivers — a great addition to the team!

Secondly, as some of you have read from the annual report, the sales arm of our business is growing! – [2] –. Upper management has decided that as of next month, Sales will operate as two departments. Pre-sales will handle customer matters before purchase. – [3] –. The department that handles after-sales and customer service will be known as Customer Support and will be headed by Paolo Fuente. We expect 10 new hires before creating the new departments.

All newcomers will be the top story in next month's company newsletter, so stay tuned! We look forward to an exciting new chapter in the history of Diligence Logistics! – [4] –.

---

25. **What is true of Ms. Robertson's time at Diligence Logistics?**

    (A) She worked as a personnel manager for eight years.

    (B) She gained expertise in customer service.

    (C) She helped expand the sales division.

    (D) She got promoted.

26. **What is suggested about Diligence Logistics?**

    (A) Pre- and after-sales are handled by the same section.

    (B) The sales department has achieved its highest profits.

    (C) New employees will work in the restructured departments.

    (D) Management will decide about the new departments next month.

27. **What will next month's newsletter focus on?**

    (A) Sales figures

    (B) Introduction of employees

    (C) A profile of the president

    (D) Customer service tips   Ⓐ Ⓑ Ⓒ Ⓓ

28. **In which of the positions marked [1], [2], [3], and [4] does the following sentence best belong?**

    "Janice Siew will lead this department."

    (A) [1]

    (B) [2]

    (C) [3]

    (D) [4]   Ⓐ Ⓑ Ⓒ Ⓓ

Shomething

Unit 6 / Shopping

Warm-up

Vocabulary

空欄に下から適切な語句を選んで書き入れなさい。なお、動詞については原形で記されています。必要に応じて適切な形に変えなさい。

1. Please contact your place of purchase for any (　　　　　　).
2. Older people are especially (　　　　　　) to cold temperatures here.
3. The pain in my foot (　　　　　　) during the night.
4. I've received a discount code for some goods, which I can use at the (　　　　　　)'s online checkout.
5. The hotel has (　　　　　　) new services for tourists from overseas.
6. This lasting high inflation will (　　　　　　) economic growth.

dampen	retailer	vulnerable
subside	refunds	roll out

TOEIC® Listening

Part 1 Photographs (22)

You will hear four short statements. Look at the picture and choose the statement that best describes what you see in the picture.

1. Ⓐ Ⓑ Ⓒ Ⓓ　　2. Ⓐ Ⓑ Ⓒ Ⓓ

Part **2** Question-Response

You will hear a question or statement and three responses. Listen carefully, and choose the best response to the question or statement.

3. Mark your answer on your answer sheet. Ⓐ Ⓑ Ⓒ

4. Mark your answer on your answer sheet. Ⓐ Ⓑ Ⓒ

5. Mark your answer on your answer sheet. Ⓐ Ⓑ Ⓒ

6. Mark your answer on your answer sheet. Ⓐ Ⓑ Ⓒ

Part **3** Conversation

You will hear a short conversation between two or more people. Listen carefully, and select the best response to each question.

7. **Who is the man shopping for?**
   (A) His assistant
   (B) His classmate
   (C) His boss
   (D) His client Ⓐ Ⓑ Ⓒ Ⓓ

8. **What does the woman suggest?**
   (A) A navy blue coat
   (B) A cream-colored hat
   (C) A pair of gloves
   (D) A silk scarf Ⓐ Ⓑ Ⓒ Ⓓ

9. **What does the man ask the woman to do?**
   (A) Deliver the item
   (B) Hold the item until later
   (C) Reduce the item's price
   (D) Wrap the item Ⓐ Ⓑ Ⓒ Ⓓ

You will hear a short talk given by a single speaker. Listen carefully, and select the best response to each question.

10. **What is mentioned about the Keystone II's cleaning power?**
    (A) It can clean a wide variety of fabrics.
    (B) It works best with heavy clothing.
    (C) It has a special mode for jackets.
    (D) It is made to get out stains. ⒶⒷⒸⒹ

11. **What does the speaker mean when she says, "You can run it all night and never know it's on"?**
    (A) The machine has longer overnight cycles.
    (B) The washer can turn on and off by itself.
    (C) The machine makes little noise.
    (D) The washer is connected to a smartphone app. ⒶⒷⒸⒹ

12. **How can a listener save on buying the Keystone II?**
    (A) By getting a coupon on the website
    (B) By looking in the newspaper for a coupon
    (C) By purchasing another appliance at the same store
    (D) By visiting an appliance store soon ⒶⒷⒸⒹ

Grammar

形容詞

　TOEIC® L&R では、空所の語彙を選択する問題の一つとして、形容詞の理解を問うものがあります。適切な形容詞を選ぶ上で、以下のことに気をつけましょう。

1. 形容詞と前置詞の関係

＜例文＞ （ⅰ）The lawyer is acquainted with bankruptcy cases.
　　　　　　　（その弁護士は倒産の案件に詳しいです。）

　　　　 （ⅱ）The company wants someone who is experienced in design.
　　　　　　　（その会社は意匠関係の経験に長けた人を求めています。）

　　　　 （ⅲ）Reza is brilliant at math.
　　　　　　　（レザは数学に長けています。）

　例文に挙げた形容詞acquainted, experienced, brilliantは、語のニュアンスの差はありますが、どの語もある知識に秀でていることを示しています。同じような意味を持つ形容詞でも、共に用いられる前置詞は決まっており、例えば、The lawyer is acquainted at bankruptcy cases. のように、形容詞acquaintedが前置詞atと共に用いられることはありません。このように形容詞と前置詞を結びつけて理解しておくことが大切です。

2. コロケーション（語と語のつながり）

＜例文＞ （ⅳ）There was a tacit understanding between staff members that they shouldn't disclose the company's future plans.
　　　　　　　（スタッフの間で、会社の将来計画を暴露してはいけないという暗黙の了解がありました。）
　　　　　　　○ silent understanding　　　○ unspoken understanding
　　　　　　　× hidden understanding　　　× covered understanding

　形容詞と名詞に限りませんが、語と語には相性の良いつながりがあります。tacit understandingは「暗黙の了解」という意味ですが、たとえhiddenやcoveredがtacitと類似の意味であっても、hidden understandingやcovered understandingとは言いません。このように、語と語の適切なつながりを覚えておく必要があります。

3. 限定用法と叙述用法の違い

＜例文＞ （ⅴ）The present owner has decided to demolish the buildings and build a parking lot on those ruins.
　　　　　　　（現在の所有者はその建物を取り壊し、跡地に駐車場を作ることを決めました。）

　　　　 （ⅵ）Caregivers must be present at the meeting on Friday.
　　　　　　　（保護者は金曜日の集会に出席する必要があります。）

　形容詞には名詞の前に置き、名詞の意味を限定する**限定用法**の形容詞と、be動詞やremainなどの不完全自動詞（＝補語を必要とする動詞）の後に置いて、動詞の意味を補う**叙述用法**の形容詞があります。どちらの用法でも同じ意味を示す形容詞も多いですが、例文（ⅴ）, （ⅵ）のように、限定用法と叙述用法で異なる意味を示す形容詞もあります。このように形容詞の使い方とその意味を合わせて理解しておくことも大切です。

Part 5 Incomplete Sentences

A word or phrase is missing in each of the sentences below. Select the best answer to complete the sentence.

13. Applicants who are not current members of the Holt Business Association will be charged an _____ fee when registering for the seminar.
    (A) easy
    (B) extra
    (C) optional
    (D) outside
    Ⓐ Ⓑ Ⓒ Ⓓ

14. With his _____ experience in computer science, Mr. Howard seems to be the most suitable candidate for the cyber security manager.
    (A) affordable
    (B) vast
    (C) cruel
    (D) inherited
    Ⓐ Ⓑ Ⓒ Ⓓ

15. Our teamwork goes quite well, simply because we have _____ interests and opinions on the next real estate project.
    (A) alike
    (B) resembling
    (C) similar
    (D) akin
    Ⓐ Ⓑ Ⓒ Ⓓ

16. Mr. Klein is _____ for the maintenance of the whole fleet of company vehicles, including the vans and buses.
    (A) dependable
    (B) possible
    (C) reliable
    (D) responsible
    Ⓐ Ⓑ Ⓒ Ⓓ

17. The sudden resignation of the chief executive put the company in a difficult and _____ position.
    (A) vulnerable
    (B) plausible
    (C) barren
    (D) formidable
    Ⓐ Ⓑ Ⓒ Ⓓ

18. The marketing head found Matt Tyson's analysis of the survey results _____ and unreasonable.
    (A) profound
    (B) superficial
    (C) thoughtful
    (D) frail
    Ⓐ Ⓑ Ⓒ Ⓓ

19. We will make _____ efforts to inform you how your personal data will be processed and used on our site.
    (A) reckless
    (B) plausible
    (C) reasonable
    (D) understandable
    Ⓐ Ⓑ Ⓒ Ⓓ

20. We in the Singapore branch are happy to offer our _____ support of the new company president.
    (A) bright
    (B) creative
    (C) hesitant
    (D) unconditional
    Ⓐ Ⓑ Ⓒ Ⓓ

Read the text that follows. A word, phrase, or sentence is missing in parts of the text. Select the best answer to complete the text.

Questions 21-24 refer to the following article.

Back to the Old Shopping Grind Again

The coronavirus pandemic was expected to turn us all into permanent online shoppers, never to set foot in physical stores again. Instead, consumers have apparently gotten tired of ordering everything _____ sitting on the sofa and have returned to shopping
                                                      21.
the old-fashioned way.

"As the pandemic has subsided, you're seeing consumers _____ back to their pre-
                                                          22.
pandemic activities," said J.G. Magee, head of a video production firm that has widely covered the retail sector in the past. "Consumers see benefits to shopping in stores."

Several factors are converging to dampen online sales growth, he said. _____. This
                                                                         23.
has led some shoppers to give up buying big-ticket discretionary items like electronics and furniture – products often purchased online – or balk at paying home-delivery fees.

Other consumers have proven eager to _____ and socialize after being cooped up at
                                        24.
home for so long during the pandemic.

"Shopping in stores is a social activity," Magee says, adding that the signs of a marked shift in consumer performances can be viewed everywhere.

---

21. (A) within
   (B) during
   (C) amid
   (D) while

   Ⓐ Ⓑ Ⓒ Ⓓ

22. (A) get
   (B) got
   (C) to get
   (D) being gotten

   Ⓐ Ⓑ Ⓒ Ⓓ

23. (A) Inflation is pressuring consumers' wallets.
   (B) The convenience of ordering is a great asset for online shop retailers.
   (C) People tend to buy bulky goods online rather than at physical stores.
   (D) Now, big bargains at local stores have brought a number of customers again.

   Ⓐ Ⓑ Ⓒ Ⓓ

24. (A) move in
   (B) get out
   (C) opt out
   (D) come off

   Ⓐ Ⓑ Ⓒ Ⓓ

Read the following texts. Select the best answer for each question.

Questions 25-29 refer to the following notice and memo.

New Recycling Collection System for Hillenbrand's Supermarket

Hillenbrand's Supermarket has rolled out a new point system to help the environment! Customers can bring empty glasses and cans, paper products and plastic products, and convert them into points via a brand-new Recycle Point Card (RPC). Customers simply need to insert their RPC into the Automatic Recycling Machine and select either metal, glass, cartons or plastic. Only certain items are eligible to be recycled, and they must be empty and clean and inserted one by one. Points will automatically be added to the card. Customers can accumulate these points to pay for any product sold in the store.

The eligible recyclables and their point values are as follows:

- Metal Cans (all sizes) — 2 points each
- 1-Liter Milk Cartons — 3 points each
- Plastic Bottles (all sizes) — 1 point each
- Glass Bottles (all sizes) — 5 points each

Sign up for your own free Recycle Point Card today!

TO: All Hillenbrand's employees
FROM: The Sales Team
RE: Incentives for New Sign-ups

Hillenbrand's new Recycle Point Card (RPC) system has been launched, but the number of customer sign-ups is still lagging. We need all employees' help in spreading the word! Did you know that the collected recyclables from our machines will be sent to a processing facility to be 100-percent recycled? By doing this, we cut our total waste by 20 percent.

For every customer sign-up, an employee can earn 250 RPC points. Get five customer sign-ups and you can receive an additional 500 RPC points.

Need more incentive? Then, how about this: The first three Hillenbrand's employees to get 30 new customer sign-ups will also win an all-expenses paid trip for two to Australia. So, let's boost those customer sign-ups today. Good luck!

25. **What is the new rewards system?**

    (A) A company policy that requires all employees to recycle

    (B) A plan that rewards employees with a trip when customers buy more

    (C) A program that rewards customers with points in exchange for recyclables

    (D) A scheme that refunds customers' money if they use less plastic

                                                    (A)　(B)　(C)　(D)

26. **What is required when using the machine?**

    (A) To insert items one at a time

    (B) To enter a membership number

    (C) To notify supermarket staff when finished

    (D) To remove any labels　　　　　　　　　　　　(A)　(B)　(C)　(D)

27. **What is NOT a feature of the new rewards system?**

    (A) It reduces waste.

    (B) Points can be used for spending.

    (C) Points will expire in a year.

    (D) There is no fee for signing up.　　　　　　　(A)　(B)　(C)　(D)

28. **What is the goal of the sales team?**

    (A) To boost customer spending

    (B) To complete the sales campaign successfully

    (C) To earn as many RPC points as possible

    (D) To increase the number of customer sign-ups　(A)　(B)　(C)　(D)

29. **Who may be able to go abroad?**

    (A) Customers who invite many people to sign up for the program

    (B) Employees who get many customers to join the program

    (C) Any employee who comes up with a great promotional slogan

    (D) The first five customers who earn 100 RPC points

                                                   (A)　(B)　(C)　(D)

7 Advertisement

Warm-up

Vocabulary

空欄に下から適切な語句を選んで書き入れなさい。なお、動詞については原形で記されています。必要に応じて適切な形に変えなさい。

1. She answered a newspaper (　　　　　) for a part-time nursing position.
2. He will be around here in 10 minutes, I (　　　　　).
3. I'm sorry I can't meet with you today; I'm (　　　　　) with my duties.
4. They raised money to help (　　　　　) children learn to read and write.
5. Several experiments are currently (　　　　　) in our lab to prove the validity of the theory.
6. A survey has (　　　　　) that a number of people are overweight.

reckon	underway	underprivileged
tied up	reveal	classified ad

TOEIC® Listening

Part 1 Photographs

You will hear four short statements. Look at the picture and choose the statement that best describes what you see in the picture.

1.
   (A) (B) (C) (D)

2.
   (A) (B) (C) (D)

Part **2** Question-Response

You will hear a question or statement and three responses. Listen carefully, and choose the best response to the question or statement.

3. Mark your answer on your answer sheet.   Ⓐ   Ⓑ   Ⓒ

4. Mark your answer on your answer sheet.   Ⓐ   Ⓑ   Ⓒ

5. Mark your answer on your answer sheet.   Ⓐ   Ⓑ   Ⓒ

6. Mark your answer on your answer sheet.   Ⓐ   Ⓑ   Ⓒ

Part **3** Conversation

You will hear a short conversation between two or more people. Listen carefully, and select the best response to each question.

7. **What type of company do the speakers work for?**
   (A) An investment company
   (B) A recruitment agency
   (C) An advertising agency
   (D) An Internet service provider   Ⓐ Ⓑ Ⓒ Ⓓ

8. **What does the woman want to try?**
   (A) Putting ads in nationwide journals
   (B) Recruiting candidates directly
   (C) Using an outside agency to find candidates
   (D) Writing a job ad herself   Ⓐ Ⓑ Ⓒ Ⓓ

9. **What benefit does Jeff mention about the woman's idea?**
   (A) It would be cheaper.
   (B) It would be more efficient.
   (C) It would please their boss.
   (D) It would take the decision out of their hands.   Ⓐ Ⓑ Ⓒ Ⓓ

Part **4** Talk

You will hear a short talk given by a single speaker. Listen carefully, and select the best response to each question.

10. **Who are the Stingers?**

(A) A baseball team

(B) A charity group

(C) A hockey team

(D) A musical band

11. **What does the speaker say about the events?**

(A) There are three events on Sunday.

(B) The events are being held to promote the musicians.

(C) Both are free and reservations are not required.

(D) One event starts in the evening.

12. **What happens tomorrow?**

(A) An article on past events will appear in a magazine.

(B) The details of the events will be in the newspaper.

(C) The orchestra will advertise the event.

(D) The fans can see the Stingers' new official website.

Grammar

1. 副詞の意味

TOEIC® L&R では空所に当てはまる適切な副詞を選ぶ問題が出題されます。文の内容を考えて副詞を選ぶ必要があります。以下の文の下線部の副詞は、間違った意味で捉えないよう注意する必要があります。

＜例文＞ （ⅰ）I wasn't at the meeting yesterday, but <u>apparently</u> it went well.
（私は昨日その会議にはいなかったんですが、おそらくうまくいったと思います。）

（ⅱ）The ABC company is <u>badly</u> in need of a new accountant.
（ABC社は新しい会計士をとても必要としています。）

（ⅲ）My friend Joe <u>barely</u> passed the exam.
（私の友人のジョーは、かろうじて試験に合格しました。）

apparently は形容詞 apparent からの類推で、「明らかに」の意味であると考えてしまう人もいるようです（例：It'll soon become apparent that he made a mistake in calculation. 彼が計算間違いをしたことは、やがて明らかになるでしょう）。副詞 apparently は「どうも…らしい」の意味で、むしろ動詞 appear と結び付けて捉える必要があります（例：It appears that the shop will be closed soon. どうやらその店はもうすぐ閉店するようです）。

badly は The interview went badly. I was so nervous.（面接はひどい結果となりました。とても緊張していたのです）のように、「ひどく」という否定的な意味を表すこともありますが、例文（ⅱ）のように、「とても」（very）の意味で用いられることもあるため、注意が必要です。

barely は rarely や seldom と同じように捉えてしまいがちですが、rarely や seldom は「ほとんど〜ない」の意味で、無いという「否定」に軸足があるのに対し、barely は「かろうじて」「わずかに」などのように「少しはある」ことを示します。She was barely 13 when she won first place in the contest.（彼女がコンテストで一等賞を取った時は、わずか13歳でした）などの例からも、barely のニュアンスが分かるのではないでしょうか。

2. 副詞による修飾

副詞は動詞や形容詞を主に修飾しますが、そのほかにも副詞が文全体を修飾するときもあります。また be 動詞の補語として使われることもあります。副詞 quite は名詞句（冠詞＋名詞）の前に置き、続く名詞句を強調する用法があります。

＜例文＞ （ⅳ）New vocabulary <u>constantly</u> appears in most languages.〈動詞を修飾〉
（ほとんどの言語で、新たな語彙が絶えず現れます。）

（ⅴ）I've got a <u>pretty</u> good idea for a new project.〈形容詞を修飾〉
（新しい企画についてかなり良い考えが浮かびました。）

（ⅵ）<u>Personally,</u> I think it's just a waste of time.〈文を修飾〉
（個人的には、それは単に時間の無駄だと思います。）

（ⅶ）I guess Sarah is <u>upstairs</u>.〈be動詞の補語〉
（サラは上の階にいると思います。）

（ⅷ）This engine makes <u>quite</u> a noise.〈名詞句を修飾〉
（このエンジンはかなりの音が出ます。）

Part 5 | Incomplete Sentences

A word or phrase is missing in each of the sentences below. Select the best answer to complete the sentence.

13. While it has already been leaked to the media, the merger of the two auto giants has not been _____ announced yet.
    (A) entirely
    (B) officially
    (C) periodically
    (D) temporarily
    Ⓐ Ⓑ Ⓒ Ⓓ

14. Be sure to have all of the tools you need and read the instructions _____ before you attempt to assemble the system.
    (A) carefully
    (B) hopefully
    (C) quietly
    (D) rarely
    Ⓐ Ⓑ Ⓒ Ⓓ

15. The government agency said that it has not _____ set a time frame for when businesses need to comply with the new regulations.
    (A) already
    (B) also
    (C) only
    (D) yet
    Ⓐ Ⓑ Ⓒ Ⓓ

16. The pop-up questionnaire will appear _____ after a customer completes their purchase and takes only a few minutes to fill out.
    (A) just
    (B) mainly
    (C) often
    (D) very
    Ⓐ Ⓑ Ⓒ Ⓓ

17. Having the copying machine in our department fixed by today is not _____ necessary, since we can take the old one out from storage and use it temporarily.
    (A) closely
    (B) absolutely
    (C) badly
    (D) consequently
    Ⓐ Ⓑ Ⓒ Ⓓ

18. As the new employee was wearing quite a casual outfit, the supervisor had to tell her to dress more _____.
    (A) attractively
    (B) intensely
    (C) professionally
    (D) strictly
    Ⓐ Ⓑ Ⓒ Ⓓ

19. Ms. Rodriguez _____ gathered the resources needed to complete the project on time, exceeding our expectations.
    (A) expectantly
    (B) observantly
    (C) privately
    (D) efficiently
    Ⓐ Ⓑ Ⓒ Ⓓ

20. The owner of Newton Gas has revealed that the firm expects profits for its household supply business to come in _____ higher over the first half of the year.
    (A) significantly
    (B) properly
    (C) economically
    (D) generously
    Ⓐ Ⓑ Ⓒ Ⓓ

Part **6** Text Completion

Read the text that follows. A word, phrase, or sentence is missing in parts of the text. Select the best answer to complete the text.

Questions 21-24 refer to the following advertisement.

GRAND RE-OPENING SALE

The Kensbury Grand Re-Opening Sale begins at 9:30 a.m. on Saturday, July 7. Kensbury will re-open after _____ remodeling. Join us for a huge day of fun – and, of
      21.
course, amazing prices across our entire range of products. In the morning, we'll have members of The Blazers professional football team out in front of our store, _____ up
                     22.
a delicious Brazilian-style barbecue for you to enjoy. _____, there will be plenty of
            23.
prizes, especially if you're one of the first few people to arrive. _____. We'll offer you
                 24.
the same sale prices online, and our warehouse crew will be working overtime to make sure you get your orders within a day or two. We feel the joy in serving you!

---

21. (A) extensive
 (B) extensively
 (C) extending
 (D) extension
   Ⓐ Ⓑ Ⓒ Ⓓ

22. (A) sizzle
 (B) sizzled
 (C) sizzles
 (D) sizzling
   Ⓐ Ⓑ Ⓒ Ⓓ

23. (A) On the contrary
 (B) Up to now
 (C) On top of that
 (D) Nevertheless
   Ⓐ Ⓑ Ⓒ Ⓓ

24. (A) Don't forget to sign up for our point card so you can get even greater discounts.
 (B) For those of you not in the area or who prefer to shop online, don't worry.
 (C) If you want an extra bargain, bring the coupon in your local newspaper.
 (D) We are delighted to announce that we have added 12 new retail shops and two upscale cafés.
   Ⓐ Ⓑ Ⓒ Ⓓ

Read the following text. Select the best answer for each question.

Questions **25-27** refer to the following advertisement.

YOUR DREAM HOME AWAITS.

As times change, so do the needs families experience in terms of housing. Few, if any, families find that the houses they once thought perfect for them are right for them a decade later. Everyone notices new features in other homes that they wish they too had.

Transform your current home into the house of your wildest dreams with a renovation by **Deutschendorf Homes**. For over 30 years, families in the greater Denver area have trusted **Deutschendorf Homes** to remodel kitchens, baths, storage areas and unfinished basements in existing homes.

A renovated room can usually be completed within one month, and the cost is reasonable. Why move to another house when your current home can be improved upon to satisfy all your needs?

Call 867-5309 and a **Deutschendorf Homes** representative will visit your home right away to assist you in preparing a design plan and securing the necessary financing permits. Finally, you'll be given a binding figure for the entire project. No cost overruns, ever.

Our guarantee: We can have construction underway within two weeks. Transforming a basic house into the home you have always dreamed of having is a trouble-free, expeditious process.

Your dream home awaits you. Don't delay — pick up the phone and call us today.

Deutschendorf Homes • 1231 Windstar Way, Denver, Colorado • 1-800-867-5309

25. What is this company advertising?

    (A) Bank loan

    (B) Remodeling homes

    (C) New properties

    (D) Furniture

26. What does this company suggest is unnecessary?

    (A) Moving to a new house

    (B) Allowing a month for work

    (C) Getting building permits

    (D) Meeting representatives in person   

27. What is NOT a part of this company's promise?

    (A) They know what permits the customer will need.

    (B) Work will begin in less than two weeks.

    (C) The project will stay within its budget.

    (D) The company only works on unfinished rooms.   

Warm-up

Vocabulary

空欄に下から適切な語句を選んで書き入れなさい。なお、動詞については原形で記されています。また、選択肢の語句は文頭に来るものも小文字で書かれています。必要に応じて適切な形に変えなさい。

1. (　　　　　　) contributes to revitalizing neighborhoods and urban development, but it also causes rent inflation.

2. She has (　　　　　　) her departure until tomorrow.

3. All the products on this website are out of our (　　　　　　).

4. Once the insurance policy (　　　　　　), it is no longer valid.

5. You will be (　　　　　　) by postal mail, if your application is successful.

6. Despite being in a dry and cold place, the plants (　　　　　　) well.

postpone	notify	thrive
expire	gentrification	price range

 TOEIC® Listening

Part **1** Photographs

You will hear four short statements. Look at the picture and choose the statement that best describes what you see in the picture.

1.
Ⓐ Ⓑ Ⓒ Ⓓ

2.

Ⓐ Ⓑ Ⓒ Ⓓ

Part **2** Question-Response

You will hear a question or statement and three responses. Listen carefully, and choose the best response to the question or statement.

3. Mark your answer on your answer sheet.   Ⓐ Ⓑ Ⓒ

4. Mark your answer on your answer sheet.   Ⓐ Ⓑ Ⓒ

5. Mark your answer on your answer sheet.   Ⓐ Ⓑ Ⓒ

6. Mark your answer on your answer sheet.   Ⓐ Ⓑ Ⓒ

Part **3** Conversation

You will hear a short conversation between two or more people. Listen carefully, and select the best response to each question.

7. **Why does the man call her?**
   (A) To renew her contract
   (B) To notify her of the approximate cost
   (C) To give information on movers
   (D) To confirm the date that she will move   Ⓐ Ⓑ Ⓒ Ⓓ

8. **What is mentioned about the moving cost?**
   (A) It was way too high last month.
   (B) The woman doesn't know the cost yet.
   (C) The moving company hasn't decided yet.
   (D) The cost will be the same as the off-peak seasons.   Ⓐ Ⓑ Ⓒ Ⓓ

9. **What does the man say about the contract?**
   (A) It had already been prepared.
   (B) The resident was in breach of contract.
   (C) It will be invalid on the day she is moving out.
   (D) It won't expire even after she leaves the property.   Ⓐ Ⓑ Ⓒ Ⓓ

Part **4** Talk

You will hear a short talk given by a single speaker. Listen carefully, and select the best response to each question.

10. **What is the program about?**
    (A) British gardens
    (B) The agricultural industry
    (C) Famous gardeners
    (D) Home gardening

11. **What does the speaker say about sunlight?**
    (A) All vegetables need lots of sunlight.
    (B) Leafy vegetables need less sunlight.
    (C) Knowledge about sunlight requirements is not important.
    (D) Fruits in general will not grow without sunlight.

12. **What does the speaker mean when he says, "let nature take its course"?**
    (A) You can let things happen without trying to control everything.
    (B) You will appreciate how beautiful nature is.
    (C) You can learn how to control weather conditions.
    (D) You'll find how easy and fun gardening is.

●注意したい前置詞の用法・意味

英語の前置詞は様々な意味で使われますが、英語を母語としない者にとっては、そのニュアンスがつかみにくいことがあります。以下に、気をつけたい前置詞の用法を挙げますので、その意味を確認しましょう。

<例文> （ⅰ）Greg is a man <u>of</u> experience.（グレッグは経験豊かな人です。）
（= Greg is an experienced man.）
（ⅱ）The weather is cold <u>for</u> this time of year.（この時期にしては寒い天候です。）
（ⅲ）The parcels are priced <u>by</u> weight.（小包は重さで値段が決まります。）
（ⅳ）I was overcharged <u>by</u> $10.（私は10ドル余分に請求されました。）
（ⅴ）That idea originated <u>with</u> Dr. Huang.（その考えはファン博士から湧き出ました。）
（ⅵ）<u>Despite</u> the bad reviews it received, his book sold well.
（良くない評価にもかかわらず、彼の本はよく売れました。）
（ⅶ）<u>During</u> her presidency, she doubled the budget for advertising.
（社長の任期中、彼女は広告予算を2倍にしました。）

例文（ⅰ）のofは特性を示すofです。他にもa woman <u>of</u> intelligence（知性ある女性）のように、ofの後には基本的には肯定的な特性を表す語が来ます。

例文（ⅱ）のforは基準と比べて、違いを際立たせるときに使われるforで、他にもShe is tall for a girl.（女の子にしては背が高い）のように使われます。

例文（ⅲ）のbyは例文のように価格を決める基準を示したり、We pay by the hour.（時間給で支払います）のように、支払いの基準を示したりといったように、何かを決める上でもとにするものを表すときに使う用法です。

例文（ⅳ）のbyは「差」を表す表現で、例文のほかにもFood prices increased <u>by</u> 15 percent in a year.（1年間で食品の価格が15%上昇しました）、I exceeded the speed limit by 20 kilometers per hour.（時速20kmの速度超過をしました）のように、増加や超過の度合いを示すときにも使われます。

例文（ⅴ）のwithは行為が行われるときの様子を表す言い方で、他にもWhy don't you wrap up the meeting <u>with</u> a presentation?（発表により、会議を終わりにしませんか）のように使います。

例文（ⅵ）のdespiteは「〜にもかかわらず」の意味ですが、in spite ofと勘違いしてofを付けないようにしましょう（例：<u>In spite of</u> his good reputation, his work performance didn't pass muster. 彼の評判はよかったのですが、彼の仕事ぶりは及第点に達していませんでした）。

例文（ⅶ）のduringは後に時間を表す表現を取る前置詞です。前置詞ですので、duringの後に分詞doing somethingの形を取ることはできません。分詞が来る場合は接続詞whileを用います（例：We chatted <u>while</u> waiting for the bus. バスを待っている間、私たちはおしゃべりしていました。×We chatted <u>during</u> waiting for the bus.）。

Part 5 Incomplete Sentences

A word or phrase is missing in each of the sentences below. Select the best answer to complete the sentence.

13. Several months after it was requested, the defective projector in the meeting room was finally replaced _____ a new one.
    (A) in
    (B) for
    (C) to
    (D) with
    Ⓐ Ⓑ Ⓒ Ⓓ

14. To celebrate their fifth anniversary, Weston's most beloved Indian restaurant is offering free children's meals _____ 5:00 and 7:00 p.m.
    (A) at
    (B) between
    (C) during
    (D) from
    Ⓐ Ⓑ Ⓒ Ⓓ

15. _____ the heavy rain, hundreds of people gathered at the outdoor event to see the famous actor.
    (A) Against
    (B) Beyond
    (C) Despite
    (D) Instead
    Ⓐ Ⓑ Ⓒ Ⓓ

16. All inspected raw materials will be stored at a location _____ from the corporate production facility.
    (A) across
    (B) against
    (C) in
    (D) along
    Ⓐ Ⓑ Ⓒ Ⓓ

17. The police announced that the number of crimes in this district had increased _____ 10 percent since last year in spite of their dedicated efforts.
    (A) for
    (B) by
    (C) in
    (D) of
    Ⓐ Ⓑ Ⓒ Ⓓ

18. All construction materials are expected to arrive seven days _____ building crews break ground.
    (A) from
    (B) during
    (C) by
    (D) before
    Ⓐ Ⓑ Ⓒ Ⓓ

19. When the employee finally handed in his report, his supervisor scolded him for the delay and warned him _____ future tardiness.
    (A) against
    (B) over
    (C) toward
    (D) within
    Ⓐ Ⓑ Ⓒ Ⓓ

20. Employees hired this month are _____ the first to participate in the computer-enhanced orientation program.
    (A) upon
    (B) throughout
    (C) with
    (D) among
    Ⓐ Ⓑ Ⓒ Ⓓ

Part 6 Text Completion

Read the text that follows. A word, phrase, or sentence is missing in parts of the text. Select the best answer to complete the text.

Questions 21-24 refer to the following article.

The volume of home deliveries has increased by nearly 60 percent in the last two years, _____ the popularity of online shopping. _____. In fact, the report says to expect the
    21.   **22.**

increase to continue at nearly 30 percent each year for the next three years. This _____
                                                                        23.

in deliveries has caused a large increase in traffic on already busy roads. What can be done to relieve this congestion? That is precisely the aim of a new government panel formed this week. The plethora of ideas that have been proposed include banning delivery vehicles on central city streets during daytime hours and _____ solar-powered
                                                                                         24.

buses instead to make deliveries.

21. (A) except for
    (B) instead of
    (C) on behalf of
    (D) thanks to

Ⓐ Ⓑ Ⓒ Ⓓ

22. (A) Online retailers are banding together to protest the limits placed on them by city governments.
    (B) The Internet began as a government project aimed at connecting computers from two distant universities.
    (C) There is no end in sight to this trend, according to a report issued by Maxim Analytics today.
    (D) To receive free shipping on your order, be sure to enter your loyalty program number in the box.

Ⓐ Ⓑ Ⓒ Ⓓ

23. (A) accuracy
    (B) drop
    (C) surge
    (D) worth

Ⓐ Ⓑ Ⓒ Ⓓ

24. (A) to use
    (B) use
    (C) used
    (D) using

Ⓐ Ⓑ Ⓒ Ⓓ

Read the following texts. Select the best answer for each question.

Questions **25-29** refer to the following advertisement, e-mail, and receipt.

Too tired to go out to eat? Craving something exotic that's far from home? Let SpeedyEats deliver whatever you want directly to your door. Your food will come fresh and piping hot...straight from the restaurant!

SpeedyEats partners with over 30 dining establishments in the city – everything from fast-food joints to ethnic food shops to Michelin-ranked hotel restaurants.*

And the best part? Our easy-to-use app for mobile phones will get you that meal in no time at all. Just register with your name, address and password. Sign up for SpeedyEats today!

** *SPECIAL ONE-TIME OFFER FOR NEW CUSTOMERS* **
ORDER OVER $25 FROM SPEEDYEATS AND RECEIVE 10% OFF.
Use coupon code **NC-10** when ordering.

Please note: SpeedyEats offers two payment options – credit card and cash. When paying in cash, please have exact change ready. For security reasons, our delivery staff do not carry money for making change.

(**Not all restaurants available in all areas at all times. Log in to the app to find the restaurants nearest you.*)

Sophia Bustamante

6 March 2023

Subject: My SpeedyEats order

To: customer-service@speedyeats.net

Hello. I was looking forward to using the SpeedyEats service since my friend sent me the ad in a text message. The app was easy to use and the food was delivered at the promised time. However, I was disappointed with one thing. When the delivery staff arrived with the food, he asked for exact change. I had only $50 cash on me at the time, and it was very inconvenient having to register my credit card on the SpeedyEats app while we were both standing there at my front door. For personal budgeting reasons, I don't use credit cards for small purchases like this. Please make it possible from now on for customers to use any amount of cash for your service.

Thank you,

Sophia Bustamante

ORDER RECEIPT		
Sri Lankan Restaurant GAMPAHA	3/5/2023	18:30
1 Crab Sri Lanka Curry	$12.00	
1 Pork String Hoppers	$20.00	
1 Kiri-Pani dessert	$10.00	
2 Mango Lassi beverage	$8.00	
Total	$50.00	
Discount	$5.00	
Delivery	$3.50	
Total due	$48.50	
To be picked up by SpeedyEats		

25. **In the advertisement, the word "craving" in paragraph 1, line 1, is closest in meaning to**

    (A) aching

    (B) commanding

    (C) seeking

    (D) withdrawing   Ⓐ Ⓑ Ⓒ Ⓓ

26. **What aspect of the service was Ms. Bustamante unhappy with?**

    (A) The delivery time

    (B) The payment policy

    (C) The application installation

    (D) The restaurant variety   Ⓐ Ⓑ Ⓒ Ⓓ

27. **When did Ms. Bustamante send the e-mail?**

    (A) The day after she ate Sri Lankan food

    (B) The day after she learned about SpeedyEats

    (C) The day after she met her friend at a restaurant

    (D) The day after she received a new credit card   Ⓐ Ⓑ Ⓒ Ⓓ

28. **What can be said of Ms. Bustamante?**

    (A) She is a first-time user of the service.

    (B) She is a restaurant reviewer.

    (C) She is a staff person at SpeedyEats.

    (D) She is new to her neighborhood.   Ⓐ Ⓑ Ⓒ Ⓓ

29. **What was the least expensive individual item Ms. Bustamante ordered?**

    (A) The dessert

    (B) The pork string hoppers

    (C) The crab curry

    (D) The drink   Ⓐ Ⓑ Ⓒ Ⓓ

Office Work

Warm-up

Vocabulary

　空欄に下から適切な語を選んで書き入れなさい。なお、動詞については原形で記されています。必要に応じて適切な形に変えなさい。

1. She (　　　　) seeds all over the garden yesterday.
2. They have approximately 350 employees on the (　　　　).
3. The organization (　　　　) a ban on advertising junk food on TV.
4. His daughter could be very (　　　　) at times.
5. The rent and food costs of the dormitory are deducted from employee (　　　　).
6. The (　　　　) has led to many small businesses going bankrupt.

demanding	recession	scatter
paychecks	advocate	payroll

TOEIC® Listening

Part 1 Photographs

　You will hear four short statements. Look at the picture and choose the statement that best describes what you see in the picture.

1.

Ⓐ Ⓑ Ⓒ Ⓓ

2.

Ⓐ Ⓑ Ⓒ Ⓓ

Part **2** Question-Response

You will hear a question or statement and three responses. Listen carefully, and choose the best response to the question or statement.

3. Mark your answer on your answer sheet.   Ⓐ Ⓑ Ⓒ

4. Mark your answer on your answer sheet.   Ⓐ Ⓑ Ⓒ

5. Mark your answer on your answer sheet.   Ⓐ Ⓑ Ⓒ

6. Mark your answer on your answer sheet.   Ⓐ Ⓑ Ⓒ

Part **3** Conversation

You will hear a short conversation between two or more people. Listen carefully, and select the best response to each question.

7. **What will Jessica do on Tuesday?**
    (A) Mail some boxes
    (B) Print some flyers
    (C) Promote some products
    (D) Register for a trade show   Ⓐ Ⓑ Ⓒ Ⓓ

8. **What is the man in charge of?**
    (A) Writing address labels
    (B) Developing a new product
    (C) Setting up a trade show booth
    (D) Designing some flyers   Ⓐ Ⓑ Ⓒ Ⓓ

9. **What will Jessica do today?**
    (A) Set up client appointments
    (B) Write the sales report with the man
    (C) Check the product description cards
    (D) Work on booth designs with the woman   Ⓐ Ⓑ Ⓒ Ⓓ

You will hear a short talk given by a single speaker. Listen carefully, and select the best response to each question.

10. **Who most likely is the speaker?**

    (A) A delivery person

    (B) A payroll employee

    (C) A warehouse manager

    (D) An international customer

11. **What will Karen most likely do next?**

    (A) Demonstrate a packing technique

    (B) Explain how to take an order

    (C) Get ready to go home

    (D) Interview the listeners

12. **What does the speaker imply when she says, "it shouldn't take too long"?**

    (A) She does not want to pay the listeners much overtime.

    (B) She knows the job tomorrow will be finished quickly.

    (C) She thinks Karen should do the extra work by herself.

    (D) She understands the listeners want to go home soon. Ⓐ Ⓑ Ⓒ Ⓓ

1. 分詞の見分け方

<例文> （ⅰ）The <u>burning</u> building belongs to his grandfather.
（その燃えている建物は、彼の祖父が所有しているものです。）

（ⅱ）The <u>weeping</u> child has lost her way.
（しくしく泣いている子どもは、道に迷っています。）

（ⅲ）Driving a car is an example of <u>learned</u> behavior.
（車の運転は、学習行動の一つの例です。）

（ⅳ）The <u>fallen</u> tree barred our way.
（倒木が、我々の行く手を阻みました。）

　分詞は、元々動詞であったものを形容詞のように使って、分詞の後に置かれた名詞の状況や特徴を述べる時に用いられます。なお、The subject <u>interesting her now</u> is linguistics.（彼女が現在興味を持っている科目は言語学です）のように、分詞を含む句が長い場合は、名詞の後に置かれます。

　TOEIC® L&RのPart 5の問題で、-ing形の分詞と-ed形の分詞を見分ける問題が出ますが、解法のコツは分詞が元々持つ「動詞の特性」に焦点を当てることです。つまり、分詞で表される部分と、その前後に生ずる名詞との関係を考える必要があります。

　例文（ⅰ）では、the buildingとburnの関係を考えると、**建物が「燃える」という行為を引き起こしており、The building is burning. の能動態の言い方になるため、-ing形の分詞が選ばれます。**例文（ⅱ）も子どもが泣くという行為を起こしているため、-ing形のweepingをchildの前に置きます。

　これに対して例文（ⅲ）は、the behavior（行動）は**学習される対象であり、the behavior is learnedのいわば受動態の関係が生まれるため、-ed形の分詞が選ばれます。**例文（ⅳ）は少しややこしいですが、現在倒れているという行為を起こしている木ではなく、台風か何かの影響で倒れてしまった木というthe tree was fallenの関係性が生じているため、-ed形のfallenを選びます。

　このように、分詞とその分詞が修飾する名詞との関係性を考えるのが、適切な分詞を選ぶコツです。

2. 動詞を修飾する分詞

　分詞はいつも名詞を修飾するわけではなく、以下のように動詞を修飾することもあります。

<例文> （ⅴ）She just kept <u>talking</u> about trivial things, even though it had been so long since we last met.
（私たちはずいぶん久しぶりに会ったのに、彼女はただ取るに足らないことを話し続けました。）

（ⅵ）The village has remained <u>unchanged</u> for over 50 years.
（その村は50年以上変わっていません。）

　動詞keepやremainは不完全自動詞であり、動詞だけでは意味が完結しません。分詞を補語として置くことにより、述部が表す内容を明らかにしています。

Part **5** Incomplete Sentences

A word or phrase is missing in each of the sentences below. Select the best answer to complete the sentence.

13. In the past two years, Juniper has become the largest retail company in the country, _____ online and in-store commerce.
    (A) dominating   (B) dominates
    (C) dominated   (D) has dominated   Ⓐ Ⓑ Ⓒ Ⓓ

14. A number of tourists lay _____ out on the floor to see the famous ceiling paintings in the museum.
    (A) stretching   (B) stretched
    (C) stretch   (D) to stretch   Ⓐ Ⓑ Ⓒ Ⓓ

15. To keep up with competing services, all orders now come with an _____ delivery date, updated in real time online.
    (A) estimate   (B) estimated
    (C) estimating   (D) estimation   Ⓐ Ⓑ Ⓒ Ⓓ

16. Because of the economic recession, IT managers are focusing more on short-term costs than long-term energy savings when _____ equipment.
    (A) purchase   (B) purchasing
    (C) purchased   (D) to purchase   Ⓐ Ⓑ Ⓒ Ⓓ

17. The latest market analysis says that consumer _____ on travel has increased by nearly 15 percent over last year.
    (A) spends   (B) spent
    (C) spending   (D) to spend   Ⓐ Ⓑ Ⓒ Ⓓ

18. _____ from all the work with her demanding clients, Emily decided to relax over the weekend.
    (A) Wear out   (B) Worn out
    (C) Wearing out   (D) Having worn out   Ⓐ Ⓑ Ⓒ Ⓓ

19. While _____, smart home devices like MySirius have created a controversy about data collection and personal privacy.
    (A) complicated   (B) convenient
    (C) delicate   (D) structured   Ⓐ Ⓑ Ⓒ Ⓓ

20. The grocery store chain is experimenting with robotic deliveries, _____ drone and driverless vehicle technologies.
    (A) considering   (B) contacting
    (C) including   (D) sampling   Ⓐ Ⓑ Ⓒ Ⓓ

Part **6** Text Completion

Read the text that follows. A word, phrase, or sentence is missing in parts of the text. Select the best answer to complete the text.

Questions 21-24 refer to the following news brief.

Wage Gap Still Prevalent, Report Finds

The CEO-worker pay gap is still a problem, according to the latest report published by The Rabe Group, a non-profit corporate watchdog. _____.

21.

CEOs of the country's largest companies now make nearly 300 times more than the average worker, a _____ from 255 times more just five years ago. On the other hand,

22.

the wage earnings of average workers _____ the same, and they feel less motivated for

23.

their work.

Rabe Group director Maria Donner says, "The economy would suffer no harm _____

24.

CEOs be paid less or taxed more." Donner also advocates for business oversight laws that would give corporate shareholders a greater say over the wage levels of a company.

---

21. (A) The Rabe Group will lead the fight for equal rights for minorities.
  (B) The report has caused problems between the government and students.
  (C) The report indicates that the gap has widened in the last five years.
  (D) The search for a new CEO for The Rabe Group continues this month.
  Ⓐ Ⓑ Ⓒ Ⓓ

23. (A) leave
  (B) remain
  (C) stand
  (D) stay
  Ⓐ Ⓑ Ⓒ Ⓓ

22. (A) peak
  (B) decline
  (C) jump
  (D) reminiscence
  Ⓐ Ⓑ Ⓒ Ⓓ

24. (A) should
  (B) than
  (C) though
  (D) when
  Ⓐ Ⓑ Ⓒ Ⓓ

Part **7** Single Passage

Read the following text. Select the best answer for each question.

Questions 25-27 refer to the following memo.

ATTENTION ALL EMPLOYEES

As Silicon Valley's newest telemarketing firm, we here at **Crystal Clear Media** (CCM) take great pride in doing our part to help reduce waste and clean up the environment.

So, pursuant to those efforts, all printer and photocopy machines will be replaced with brand-new models starting next Monday morning. These new machines will allow us to:

◆ Use less ink: Each paper printout uses 30 percent less ink than the old machines.
◆ Conserve energy: When not in use, the power automatically turns off.
◆ Record monthly data: A detailed monthly report of each department's printer usage will be generated.

We need everybody to get on board and do their share! Did you know that we used single-sided printing on 80 percent of documents last year? If we had set the printer to double-sided printing, we could have saved at least 60 trees! We ask that you use double-sided printing for most or all of your documents from now on.

All staff are required to attend a training session next week. The training will focus on how to set up and format your devices to the new machines as well as some trouble-shooting procedures in case the new machines ever go on the blink.

Choose one session:
____Monday, April 22, 9:00 a.m.-10:00 a.m.
____Wednesday, April 24, 12:00 noon-1:00 p.m.
____Friday, April 26, 5:00 p.m.-6:00 p.m.

Consult with your department head for further information. And thank you for doing your part at **Crystal Clear Media** — it really does make a difference!

25. **What can be said about the new machines?**

    (A) They are efficient.

    (B) They are inexpensive.

    (C) They are speedy.

    (D) They are the most advanced.   Ⓐ Ⓑ Ⓒ Ⓓ

26. **Why was last year's printing percentage mentioned?**

    (A) To show that the new machines are not eco-friendly

    (B) To discourage printing in color

    (C) To encourage more frequent maintenance to save ink

    (D) To highlight how to prevent excess paper use   Ⓐ Ⓑ Ⓒ Ⓓ

27. **What will the training session NOT cover?**

    (A) How to link laptops to the printers

    (B) How to handle printer troubles

    (C) How to analyze all printer data

    (D) How to format the device to connect to new printers   Ⓐ Ⓑ Ⓒ Ⓓ

Business

Warm-up

Vocabulary

空欄に下から適切な語を選んで書き入れなさい。なお、動詞については原形で記されています。必要に応じて適切な形に変えなさい。

1. You should save your working file frequently as a (　　　　) against computer failure.
2. Roughly 150 guests attended the state (　　　　) at Buckingham Palace yesterday.
3. In the case of bankruptcy, (　　　　) can lose up to their entire investment.
4. Brisbane made a successful (　　　　) to host the 2032 Olympic games.
5. The newspaper (　　　　) two pages to the advertisement of newly published books.
6. Political leaders and business (　　　　) discussed economic issues at the conference.

shareholders	dedicate	banquet
precaution	bid	executives

TOEIC® Listening

Part 1 Photographs (38)

You will hear four short statements. Look at the picture and choose the statement that best describes what you see in the picture.

1.

Ⓐ Ⓑ Ⓒ Ⓓ

2.

Ⓐ Ⓑ Ⓒ Ⓓ

Part **2** Question-Response

You will hear a question or statement and three responses. Listen carefully, and choose the best response to the question or statement.

3. Mark your answer on your answer sheet. Ⓐ Ⓑ Ⓒ

4. Mark your answer on your answer sheet. Ⓐ Ⓑ Ⓒ

5. Mark your answer on your answer sheet. Ⓐ Ⓑ Ⓒ

6. Mark your answer on your answer sheet. Ⓐ Ⓑ Ⓒ

Part **3** Conversation

You will hear a short conversation between two or more people. Listen carefully, and select the best response to each question.

7. **Who will sit at the round tables?**
   (A) New employees
   (B) The guest speakers
   (C) The presenters
   (D) Top-level employees   Ⓐ Ⓑ Ⓒ Ⓓ

8. **Look at the graphic. Which table will most likely seat 13 people?**
   (A) 1
   (B) 2
   (C) 3
   (D) 4

   Ⓐ Ⓑ Ⓒ Ⓓ

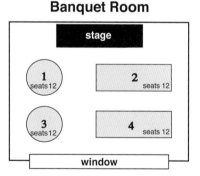

Banquet Room

9. **What does the woman say she will be doing at the banquet?**
   (A) Filling beverage glasses
   (B) Hosting it
   (C) Serving food
   (D) Speaking with co-workers   Ⓐ Ⓑ Ⓒ Ⓓ

You will hear a short talk given by a single speaker. Listen carefully, and select the best response to each question.

10. **What did consumers spend the most money on last quarter?**
    (A) Housing
    (B) Shopping
    (C) Taxes
    (D) Transportation   Ⓐ Ⓑ Ⓒ Ⓓ

11. **What might cause consumer spending to decrease next quarter?**
    (A) A decrease in population
    (B) Fewer retail outlets
    (C) A higher tax rate
    (D) Lower incomes   Ⓐ Ⓑ Ⓒ Ⓓ

12. **What will listeners hear next?**
    (A) An advertisement
    (B) An analysis of business trends
    (C) A government official's speech
    (D) A report on the president's policies   Ⓐ Ⓑ Ⓒ Ⓓ

Grammar

接続詞・関係詞

このユニットの文法項目は接続詞と関係詞ですが、特に接続詞について説明します。

●**接続詞と前置詞**

<例文> （ⅰ）Small businesses say they likely won't survive <u>unless</u> they satisfy their customers in various ways.
（小企業は、様々な方法で顧客を満足させない限り、存続できないと言っています。）

（ⅱ）<u>Since</u> we've got a few minutes before the next meeting, why don't you have a cup of coffee?
（次の会議まで数分時間ができたので、コーヒーを飲みませんか。）

（ⅲ）You can join the party, <u>provided</u> you pay for your own meal.
（食事代を自分で払うのなら、パーティーに参加しても構いませんよ。）

（ⅳ）Joe ate a bunch of food for lunch, <u>whereas</u> his wife Kate had just a sandwich.
（ジョーは昼食をずいぶんたくさん食べましたが、彼の妻のケイトはサンドイッチしか食べていません。）

（ⅴ）This is one possible solution; <u>however</u>, there must be others.
（これは一つの可能な解決法です。しかし、きっと他の方法もあるはずです。）

（ⅵ）I attended the meeting, <u>though</u> I had a fever.
（熱がありましたが、会議に出席しました。）

　例文（ⅰ）〜（ⅵ）の下線部は接続詞で、節と節を結んでいます。接続詞はand, but, orのように句と句を結ぶものもありますが、例文で取り上げた接続詞は節の前に置いて、他の節との間の様々な意味関係を表します。

　接続詞ではなく前置詞を用いて、節との関係を表す場合があります。例文を見てみましょう。

<例文> （ⅶ）<u>Unlike</u> conventional libraries, you can drink in here.
（昔の図書館とは違って、ここでは飲み物を飲んでも構いません。）

（ⅷ）Do you speak any other languages <u>besides</u> French and German?
（フランス語とドイツ語の他にも何か言語を話せますか。）

（ⅸ）<u>Despite</u> all his efforts, he couldn't change her mind.
（彼はいろいろ努力しましたが、彼女の気持ちを変えることはできませんでした。）

　例文（ⅶ）〜（ⅸ）は、前置詞から始まる前置詞句が使われています。前置詞の後は名詞句が来ており、節ではありません。

　TOEIC® L&RのPart 5あるいはPart 6で適切な接続詞を選ぶものがありますが、空所の後が節になっている場合は、前置詞ではなく接続詞を選ばなければなりません。このように、空所の後が節になっているか句になっているかを見分けるのも、適切な接続詞を選ぶ上での基準になります。

Part 5 Incomplete Sentences

A word or phrase is missing in each of the sentences below. Select the best answer to complete the sentence.

13. _____ the coffee manufacturer launches its new instant coffee line nationwide, it plans to host a concert as a marketing event.
    (A) Although   (B) As
    (C) Whether   (D) Except that   Ⓐ Ⓑ Ⓒ Ⓓ

14. _____ you're planning a large corporate banquet or a smaller business lunch, think of Gregson Catering.
    (A) Because   (B) Though
    (C) Whether   (D) While   Ⓐ Ⓑ Ⓒ Ⓓ

15. Please let us know if you have any trouble _____ staying in Inverness.
    (A) during   (B) as soon as
    (C) provided   (D) while   Ⓐ Ⓑ Ⓒ Ⓓ

16. _____ small, the new apartment building by Westwood Housing Co. is well designed and easy to access from the downtown area.
    (A) Although   (B) Despite
    (C) Since   (D) Unless   Ⓐ Ⓑ Ⓒ Ⓓ

17. _____ the company next door has moved, we should carry out our plan of many years to expand our office.
    (A) Now that   (B) Suppose
    (C) Whenever   (D) While   Ⓐ Ⓑ Ⓒ Ⓓ

18. We'll buy everything that Arlington Electronics produces, _____ the price is right.
    (A) although   (B) even if
    (C) provided   (D) once   Ⓐ Ⓑ Ⓒ Ⓓ

19. Glass Art Crafters, _____ Rick Gonzales was trained in specialized glassmaking techniques, has declared bankruptcy.
    (A) that   (B) which
    (C) what   (D) where   Ⓐ Ⓑ Ⓒ Ⓓ

20. We are sure that the Bay Beach Hotel will provide the perfect resting place for you on your journey, _____ your reason for visiting Cape Town.
    (A) whoever   (B) whatever
    (C) wherever   (D) however   Ⓐ Ⓑ Ⓒ Ⓓ

Part **6** Text Completion

Read the text that follows. A word, phrase, or sentence is missing in parts of the text. Select the best answer to complete the text.

Questions 21-24 refer to the following notice.

The purpose of this website is to _____ people the information they need to appreciate
                                                 21.

the value of and make educated decisions about insurance. With more than 60 insurance
company-affiliated members — including regional, national and global carriers — we
are the largest source of insurance information on the Internet. Our website, blog and
social media channels offer a profusion of data-driven studies, videos, articles and
infographics solely _____ to enhancing knowledge about insurance. We neither lobby
                                    22.

for nor sell insurance. _____. If your business, organization or educational institution is
                            23.

interested in _____ with our website, please contact us.
            24.

21. (A) provide
    (B) share
    (C) give
    (D) lend
        Ⓐ Ⓑ Ⓒ Ⓓ

22. (A) dedicate
    (B) dedicated
    (C) dedicates
    (D) dedicating
        Ⓐ Ⓑ Ⓒ Ⓓ

23. (A) Thus, we are ready to show you the best insurance you should buy.
    (B) Hence, you can rest assured about using this website.
    (C) As you know, the terms and conditions of insurance are so complicated.
    (D) We are happy to announce our decision on amalgamation.
        Ⓐ Ⓑ Ⓒ Ⓓ

24. (A) collaborate
    (B) collaborating
    (C) collaborative
    (D) collaboratively
        Ⓐ Ⓑ Ⓒ Ⓓ

Read the following text. Select the best answer for each question.

Questions 25-27 refer to the following press release.

TECHNIQ CHOOSES RIVERDALE FOR NEW PLANT

RIVERDALE — Sacramento-based microchip manufacturer Techniq Enterprises announced today its plans to open a new manufacturing facility in Riverdale. The new facility will produce Techniq's newest line of Dynamix microchips. —[1]—. Once up and running, the facility is expected to employ about 300 people.

Techniq carefully surveyed dozens of potential locations, finally narrowing the choice down to three: Riverdale, Sharpsburg and Peterskill. —[2]—. "Riverdale won us over with its generous tax breaks, not to mention its highly educated workforce," said CEO Dr. Muhammad Khan. "It also helped that a large research university is nearby."

—[3]—. Dynamix microchips have been manufactured on a temporary basis at Techniq's Simi Valley plant, which is expected to return to its primary mission of producing semiconductors once the new plant becomes operational in July. —[4]—.

---

25. **What is the purpose of the press release?**
    (A) To promote a new product line
    (B) To announce an expansion
    (C) To explain a corporate merger
    (D) To request bids for a competition

26. **What is NOT indicated about Techniq Enterprises?**

    (A) It has a facility in Simi Valley.

    (B) Its headquarters is in Sacramento.

    (C) It will release a new product in July.

    (D) It makes semiconductors.   Ⓐ Ⓑ Ⓒ Ⓓ

27. **In which of the positions marked [1], [2], [3], and [4] does the following sentence best belong?**

    "It will be housed in the former Philbert Electronics assembly complex."

    (A) [1]

    (B) [2]

    (C) [3]

    (D) [4]   Ⓐ Ⓑ Ⓒ Ⓓ

Traffic

Warm-up

Vocabulary

空欄に下から適切な語を選んで書き入れなさい。なお、動詞については原形で記されています。必要に応じて適切な形に変えなさい。

1. The company endured through a period of (　　　　　) after the merger.
2. My dad (　　　　) that he might pay for my trip to Boston.
3. A surprise (　　　　　) me on my birthday — I got proposed to.
4. My girlfriend didn't call or (　　　　　) me all day. She must be angry.
5. The oil price has (　　　　) by 15 percent.
6. During the summer break, I got (　　　　　) on watching games of the high school baseball tournament.

hint	plummet	hooked
await	turbulence	text

TOEIC® Listening

Part **1** Photographs

You will hear four short statements. Look at the picture and choose the statement that best describes what you see in the picture.

1.

Ⓐ Ⓑ Ⓒ Ⓓ

2.

Ⓐ Ⓑ Ⓒ Ⓓ

Part 2 Question-Response

You will hear a question or statement and three responses. Listen carefully, and choose the best response to the question or statement.

3. Mark your answer on your answer sheet.   Ⓐ Ⓑ Ⓒ

4. Mark your answer on your answer sheet.   Ⓐ Ⓑ Ⓒ

5. Mark your answer on your answer sheet.   Ⓐ Ⓑ Ⓒ

6. Mark your answer on your answer sheet.   Ⓐ Ⓑ Ⓒ

Part 3 Conversation

You will hear a short conversation between two or more people. Listen carefully, and select the best response to each question.

7. **Who are the speakers?**
    (A) Colleagues
    (B) Friends
    (C) Husband and wife
    (D) Mother and son   Ⓐ Ⓑ Ⓒ Ⓓ

8. **Why does the woman recommend the man to use public transportation?**
    (A) Weekdays are always crowded.
    (B) The traffic is dying down.
    (C) It is less expensive.
    (D) He could be caught in traffic.   Ⓐ Ⓑ Ⓒ Ⓓ

9. **What does the woman give to the man?**
    (A) A timetable
    (B) A phone
    (C) A map
    (D) A key   Ⓐ Ⓑ Ⓒ Ⓓ

You will hear a short talk given by a single speaker. Listen carefully, and select the best response to each question.

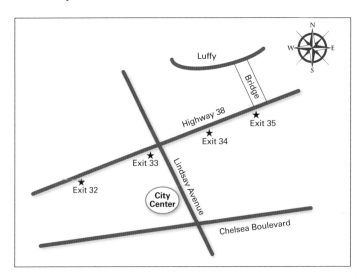

10.   Look at the map. Which exit is closest to the City Center for drivers?

(A) Exit 32

(B) Exit 33

(C) Exit 34

(D) Exit 35   Ⓐ Ⓑ Ⓒ Ⓓ

11.   Why does the speaker mention Chelsea Boulevard?

(A) It has a lot of traffic on it.

(B) It is under construction.

(C) It is an alternative to the highway.

(D) It leads to Lindsay Avenue.   Ⓐ Ⓑ Ⓒ Ⓓ

12.   What does the speaker recommend to those heading to Luffy?

(A) Take Lindsay Avenue

(B) Take the subway

(C) Use a shuttle bus

(D) Use the highway   Ⓐ Ⓑ Ⓒ Ⓓ

Grammar

仮定法

1. 直説法と仮定法

＜例文＞ （ⅰ）If it rains tomorrow, I'll stay home and chill out.　　　　〈直説法〉
　　　　　　（明日雨が降れば、家でゆっくりします。）

　　　　 （ⅱ）If I were in your place, I would tell her the truth.　　　　〈仮定法〉
　　　　　　（もし私があなたの立場なら、彼女に真実を告げます。）

　　　　 （ⅲ）If I had known of the train strike, I would have driven to the office.〈仮定法〉
　　　　　　（電車のストライキを知っていれば、車で会社に行きました。）

　英語では「もし～だったら」と言う場合に、その事柄が現実に起こるかどうかに基づいて言い方を変えます。現実に起こる場合は「直説法」の形が使われるのに対し、実際には起こらないことや、あくまでも現実とは異なることについて述べる場合は「仮定法」が用いられます。
　仮定法の場合は、if節内の動詞の時制を一つ下げて（一つ前の時制にして）、今の時間軸と異なる話、すなわち仮定の話であることを明確にします。また、主節に would, could, might のような助動詞を用いて、あくまでも仮定の話であることを示します。
　例文（ⅰ）はif節で示した内容が実際に起こると思って話をしているのに対し、例文（ⅱ）,（ⅲ）はif節の内容は「実際にはないこと」として話しています。つまり、自分とは異なる人間になることはできませんし、ストライキも全く知らなかったことを示しています。例文（ⅱ）は今の話、例文（ⅲ）は過去の話であることが、if節内の動詞の形から分かります。

2. if節を用いない仮定法

　if節とは異なる言い方をする仮定法や、if節を用いない仮定法もあります。以下のものは、その例です。

＜例文＞ （ⅳ）<u>Should you have any questions</u>, please don't hesitate to ask.
　　　　　　（万一質問があれば、遠慮せずにお尋ねください。）

　　　　 （ⅴ）<u>Were we to offer you the job</u>, would you take it?
　　　　　　（仮にその仕事をあなたにお願いすれば、引き受けてくださいますか。）

　　　　 （ⅵ）<u>With more money</u>, I could get a new computer.
　　　　　　（もっとお金があれば、新しいコンピュータが買えるのですが。）

　　　　 （ⅶ）<u>Without the grant</u>, I couldn't have done this research.
　　　　　　（助成金がなければ、この研究はできなかったでしょう。）

　　　　 （ⅷ）<u>But for you</u>, I couldn't have started up this business.
　　　　　　（あなたがいなければ、この事業を始めることは不可能だったでしょう。）

　　　　 （ⅸ）I think <u>it would be better to do it right now</u>.
　　　　　　（今すぐやったほうがよいと思いますよ。）

　例文（ⅳ）～（ⅸ）の下線部は、「もしそのような状況であれば」ということを様々な言い方で述べています。例文（ⅳ）のように、主節に助動詞を用いない言い方もあります。
　例文（ⅸ）は助動詞 would を用いて発言を和らげる効果を生んでおり、絶対的な提案でないことを示しています。

TOEIC® Reading

Part **5** Incomplete Sentences

A word or phrase is missing in each of the sentences below. Select the best answer to complete the sentence.

13. Matthew would never _____ that he was wrong if you hadn't told him.
    (A) realize
    (B) have realized
    (C) be realized
    (D) have been realized   Ⓐ Ⓑ Ⓒ Ⓓ

14. My friend Ellie wishes she _____ her mobile phone, but she is really hooked on texting and she definitely can't.
    (A) can get rid of
    (B) could get rid of
    (C) could have gotten rid of
    (D) had gotten rid of   Ⓐ Ⓑ Ⓒ Ⓓ

15. _____ your excellent advice, my proposal for the next project would not have been accepted.
    (A) With
    (B) Should
    (C) But for
    (D) If not   Ⓐ Ⓑ Ⓒ Ⓓ

16. Had we known about the stock shortage, we _____ at a loss like this.
    (A) won't be
    (B) wouldn't be
    (C) wouldn't have been
    (D) haven't been   Ⓐ Ⓑ Ⓒ Ⓓ

17. Our boss demanded that we _____ at the office before 6 p.m. today.
    (A) be back
    (B) will be back
    (C) are to be back
    (D) were to be back   Ⓐ Ⓑ Ⓒ Ⓓ

18. Don't enter the wrong password so many times, _____ the website will lock you out.
    (A) if
    (B) provided
    (C) so that
    (D) otherwise   Ⓐ Ⓑ Ⓒ Ⓓ

19. _____ we double-checked the figures of the document, we would have noticed the mistake in calculation.
    (A) When
    (B) If
    (C) Unless
    (D) Had   Ⓐ Ⓑ Ⓒ Ⓓ

20. If you had told me that you were going to be late in coming, I _____ some more.
    (A) could sleep in
    (B) couldn't sleep in
    (C) could have slept in
    (D) couldn't have slept in   Ⓐ Ⓑ Ⓒ Ⓓ

Part **6** Text Completion

Read the text that follows. A word, phrase, or sentence is missing in parts of the text. Select the best answer to complete the text.

Questions 21-24 refer to the following article.

New Bike Rental App

Jerseyville residents, get ready for the latest mobile app. This one lets you _____

                                                      21.

bicycles from central points around the city for 5 euros per hour and return them the same day. The city has allowed several bike rental companies, BikePath and e-Wheels among them, to place several dozen bikes around the city, with the agreement that the companies will maintain the bikes. _____. _____ the mobile app, riders can unlock the

                                          22.   **23.**

bike, ride it for as long as they like and then pay at the end of their trip. BikePath even has electric-assist bikes that help riders get up those _____ Jerseyville hills. More

                                               24.

information can be obtained at the municipal website: *www.jerseyville.gov*

---

21. (A) exchange
    (B) loan
    (C) borrow
    (D) rent

                    Ⓐ Ⓑ Ⓒ Ⓓ

22. (A) Bike repair has become a big business in Jerseyville, with several new shops opening recently.
    (B) Our line of bicycles comes in bright colors, so they are often stolen.
    (C) The companies have also agreed to take care of bicycles that are left in inappropriate places.
    (D) Tourists are looking for cheaper ways to get around the city, so scooters could be the answer.

                    Ⓐ Ⓑ Ⓒ Ⓓ

23. (A) Using
    (B) Use
    (C) Used
    (D) Having used

                    Ⓐ Ⓑ Ⓒ Ⓓ

24. (A) broad
    (B) inclined
    (C) narrow
    (D) steep

                    Ⓐ Ⓑ Ⓒ Ⓓ

Part **7** Multiple Passages

Read the following texts. Select the best answer for each question.

Questions 25-29 refer to the following article and review.

Business — 12A   **Metropolitan Star-Tribune**

Puma Poised to Boost Devon Motors Sales

Devon Motors hinted that its long-awaited new hatchback, Puma, will be released this spring. Critics and fans of the company alike are eagerly awaiting Devon Motors' entry into the compact-car market. If it has any of the current Devon Motors styling, it should be hot! Long known for its flashy, gas-guzzling SUVs and trucks, Devon Motors has seen its sales plummet as gas prices have risen and consumers shifted to smaller, more fuel-efficient vehicles. Devon Motors expects the Puma to help the company break into the small-car market, which up to now has been largely dominated by imports.

Review: Puma — Devon Motors
★★★★☆

The Puma was designed to grab your attention and that it does, in more ways than one. Start with the styling: Its bold lines and sporty appearance make it stand out from the usually boring design of most hatchbacks. In fact, it resembles a sports car more than a compact station wagon.

The 155-horsepower engine is not huge, but it does offer plenty of power for such a small car. And while it may look like a sports car, it doesn't quite handle like one. Still, it was fun to drive. It has a roomy interior, five seats and offers plenty of space in the trunk.

The Puma has decent fuel economy. With an estimated 32 miles per gallon on the highway and 28 miles per gallon in the city, it's not the best in its class. But it is better than any of Devon Motors' other cars and SUVs, not to mention its gas-guzzling trucks.

This is Devon Motors' first step into the small-car market. I predict that we'll see better fuel efficiency in future versions of this car as well as their other new, smaller models.

With a starting price of $15,935, it's not the cheapest in its class, but then again, it's still very affordable. I expect this car will appeal to young people buying their first car. They are the number-one buyers for compact hatchbacks.

The independent automobile testing association Riley Testing gave the Puma four out of five stars for predicted reliability — not bad, especially for a company that has recently gotten a reputation for unreliable vehicles.

We give Puma four stars too.

— J. C. Grange

CAR AFFICIONADO Magazine   2023 Spring edition

---

25. **What is the article mainly about?**

    (A) Changes in imported cars

    (B) A new car company

    (C) Trends in truck design

    (D) A new model of car   Ⓐ Ⓑ Ⓒ Ⓓ

26. **What does the reviewer say about the Puma?**

    (A) It will appeal mostly to sports fans.

    (B) It has a lot of trunk space.

    (C) It is overpriced compared to imports.

    (D) It offers outstanding fuel efficiency.   Ⓐ Ⓑ Ⓒ Ⓓ

27. **Why did Devon Motors decide to start making smaller cars?**

    (A) To produce less expensive cars

    (B) To increase sales overseas

    (C) To respond to consumer demand

    (D) To improve its reputation for reliability   Ⓐ Ⓑ Ⓒ Ⓓ

28. **What can be inferred about first-time car buyers?**

    (A) They will be unable to afford the Puma.

    (B) Many of them buy imported compact hatchbacks.

    (C) They like cars with lots of seating options.

    (D) They are only interested in styling and appearance.   Ⓐ Ⓑ Ⓒ Ⓓ

29. **How is the Puma different from other Devon Motors cars?**

    (A) It is more expensive.

    (B) It gets better gas mileage.

    (C) It appeals to young adults.

    (D) It is a compact sedan.   Ⓐ Ⓑ Ⓒ Ⓓ

Finance and Banking

Warm-up

Vocabulary

空欄に下から適切な語句を選んで書き入れなさい。なお、動詞については原形で記されています。また、選択肢の語句は文頭に来るものも小文字で書かれています。必要に応じて適切な形に変えなさい。

1. Tomato prices are (   ) due to adverse weather.
2. (   ) shoppers make a list of what they need before heading to the store so as to avoid making impulse purchases.
3. You may (   ) of the company's pension plan.
4. The disaster will have a (   ) impact on the economy.
5. What the boss is saying doesn't make (   ) at all.
6. We stayed in a wonderfully (   ) old log cabin on the school trip.

savvy	soar	rustic
devastating	sense	opt out

TOEIC® Listening

Part **1** Photographs

You will hear four short statements. Look at the picture and choose the statement that best describes what you see in the picture.

1.

   Ⓐ Ⓑ Ⓒ Ⓓ

2.

   Ⓐ Ⓑ Ⓒ Ⓓ

Part **2** Question-Response

You will hear a question or statement and three responses. Listen carefully, and choose the best response to the question or statement.

3. Mark your answer on your answer sheet.   (A) (B) (C)

4. Mark your answer on your answer sheet.   (A) (B) (C)

5. Mark your answer on your answer sheet.   (A) (B) (C)

6. Mark your answer on your answer sheet.   (A) (B) (C)

Part **3** Conversation

You will hear a short conversation between two or more people. Listen carefully, and select the best response to each question.

7. **Why does the woman want to buy a house?**
    (A) She has no place to live.
    (B) She likes the atmosphere of Milwaukee.
    (C) She doesn't want to leave all her money in the bank.
    (D) She will inherit her parents' property.   (A) (B) (C) (D)

8. **What does the man say about the woman's workplace?**
    (A) Her workplace is close to Milwaukee.
    (B) The woman lives close to her office.
    (C) Her parents live near the woman's workplace.
    (D) Her workplace is far from Milwaukee.   (A) (B) (C) (D)

9. **What does the woman plan to do after buying the house?**
    (A) She will live there.
    (B) She will collect rent.
    (C) She will move in with her parents.
    (D) She will rent an apartment.   (A) (B) (C) (D)

You will hear a short talk given by a single speaker. Listen carefully, and select the best response to each question.

10. **What have employers done during the recession?**
    (A) Cut some personnel
    (B) Lowered employees' salaries
    (C) Paid huge amounts of money to their clients
    (D) Placed a great burden on themselves Ⓐ Ⓑ Ⓒ Ⓓ

11. **Why docs the speaker mention people with families?**
    (A) To stress how hard it is to make a living
    (B) To indicate the difficulty of paying for education
    (C) To explain the importance of investing in stocks
    (D) To help others understand the financial crisis Ⓐ Ⓑ Ⓒ Ⓓ

12. **What does René Erlanger recommend?**
    (A) To find more a profitable line of work
    (B) To find a company with good benefits
    (C) To take a long vacation
    (D) To be prudent in handling one's finances Ⓐ Ⓑ Ⓒ Ⓓ

Grammar

数量詞

1. 数量詞 all と every

<例文>（ⅰ）All students in this class are really good.
　　　　（このクラスの学生は皆よくできます。）
　　　　（ⅱ）Every student in this class is really good.
　　　　（このクラスはどの学生もとてもよくできます。）

　数量詞 all と every はどちらも「すべて」を表す語ですが、all は総称的に捉えているのに対し、every は個々の成員を際立たせたうえで、まとめて表す場合に好んで用いられます。

　よって、例文（ⅰ）の場合は、クラス全体を捉えてクラスの様子を述べているのに対し、例文（ⅱ）の場合は、クラスの学生それぞれが優秀で、一人一人を念頭に置いて言っているという違いがあります。

　例文（ⅲ）にある every single の表現では、このことがよりよく分かります。

<例文>（ⅲ）Don't jot down every single word I say.
　　　　（私の言うことばをどの語も漏らさず書き記すようなことはしないでくださいね。）

2. 数量詞 some と any

　数量詞 some を使う時は、話者は、ある一定のものあるいは一定の範囲を念頭に置いて話をしています。これに対し、any は一定のものや範囲を念頭に置いていません。次の例文（ⅳ）,（ⅴ）にこの違いが表れています。

<例文>（ⅳ）You can take some of them from here.
　　　　（ここからいくつか持って行ってもいいですよ。）
　　　　（ⅴ）You can take any of them from here.
　　　　（ここからどれを持って行ってもいいですよ。）

　例文（ⅳ）ではここにあるものからいくつか持って行ってよいことを示しており、話者は全部持って行くことは想定していません。一方、例文（ⅴ）の場合は、どれでも持って行ってよいことを示しており、仮に全部持って行ったとしても問題ないと言えます。
　このことから、相手に飲み物を勧めるときなどには、何か飲んでもらうことを想定しているため、例文（ⅵ）のように some を主体とした言い方が好まれます。

<例文>（ⅵ）Would you like something to drink?　（何かお飲み物はいかがでしょうか。）

Part **5** Incomplete Sentences

A word or phrase is missing in each of the sentences below. Select the best answer to complete the sentence.

13. I had to go to New York _____ single week until last year, but now we have online meetings instead.

    (A) all   (B) each

    (C) every   (D) either   Ⓐ Ⓑ Ⓒ Ⓓ

14. Mr. Kelly needed to book _____ room for his colleague but was unsure what type of room the man would prefer.

    (A) another   (B) either

    (C) much   (D) other   Ⓐ Ⓑ Ⓒ Ⓓ

15. _____ of his restaurants has a different menu, and the one in this town has a great selection of pasta.

    (A) Every   (B) Each

    (C) Either   (D) Some   Ⓐ Ⓑ Ⓒ Ⓓ

16. You don't need to worry; _____ employee in your firm caused any trouble with your clients.

    (A) neither   (B) none

    (C) no   (D) few   Ⓐ Ⓑ Ⓒ Ⓓ

17. Mr. Richards was finally forced to tell his assistant what _____ people in the company know: he was retiring in six months.

    (A) any   (B) few

    (C) much   (D) such   Ⓐ Ⓑ Ⓒ Ⓓ

18. Unfortunately, _____ large number of book retailers went out of business over the last 10 years, due to flourishing online booksellers.

    (A) a   (B) the

    (C) all   (D) every   Ⓐ Ⓑ Ⓒ Ⓓ

19. Almost _____ bottle of wine was broken, so I had to place an order again.

    (A) all   (B) any

    (C) every   (D) no   Ⓐ Ⓑ Ⓒ Ⓓ

20. Due to her duties as project manager, there were certainly quite a _____ nights when she couldn't sleep well.

    (A) many   (B) number

    (C) lot   (D) few   Ⓐ Ⓑ Ⓒ Ⓓ

Part **6** Text Completion

Read the text that follows. A word, phrase, or sentence is missing in parts of the text. Select the best answer to complete the text.

Questions 21-24 refer to the following article.

Using Financial Awareness to Reach the Community

These are turbulent times for banks, which have had both profits and reputations hurt by the recent financial crisis and _____. Regaining customer trust and generating positive
21.
press coverage are priorities for banks, big and small, which are finding that one way to generate good will is through financial literacy programs.

Jorge Fitch, financial education program manager at First Nation Trust Bank, spearheads the bank's financial literacy efforts, _____ out in particular to youth and minority groups
22.
in society. _____.
23.

Fitch, who began as a bank teller almost two decades ago, said education is so important because "financial knowledge is _____." He adds, "Just hoping that everything will
24.
somehow work out well is no way to manage your finances."

---

21. (A) denial
  (B) recession
  (C) concatenation
  (D) growth
   Ⓐ Ⓑ Ⓒ Ⓓ

23. (A) These people know the ins and outs of finance and use banks so often.
  (B) His considerable expertise in finance is invaluable for entrepreneurs.
  (C) Surveys show these populations want to know more about checking accounts, taxes and credit cards.
  (D) Money can bring out the best or worst in any person.
   Ⓐ Ⓑ Ⓒ Ⓓ

22. (A) reach
  (B) reached
  (C) to reach
  (D) reaching
   Ⓐ Ⓑ Ⓒ Ⓓ

24. (A) power
  (B) disaster
  (C) redundant
  (D) supplementary
   Ⓐ Ⓑ Ⓒ Ⓓ

Read the following texts. Select the best answer for each question.

Questions 25-29 refer to the following memo and e-mail.

MEMORANDUM

TO: All Staff
FROM: Tom R. Benally, Vice President, Operations
DATE: January 15, 2024
SUBJECT: Retirement Plan

On the advice of Dr. Li Bachmai, a top-ranking consultant hired to advise us as to the best way to improve employee benefits, the company will be implementing this year a new retirement plan for all employees.

Each year, employees will make a mandatory contribution to the retirement fund equal to 10% of their annual salary. These payments will be matched, dollar for dollar, by the company, and the fund will be used to ensure that all employees have a generous pension package when they retire.

Employees will be eligible to start drawing a pension after contributing to the retirement fund for 10 years.

Benefits increase for every three years of contribution thereafter, maxing out at 21 years. Employees who pay into the program for more than 15 years and who are forced to retire because of mandatory retirement-age laws will automatically receive maximum benefits. Employees who leave the firm before they have worked here long enough to qualify for a pension will receive the amount they have contributed as a lump-sum payment upon leaving.

Please contact the director of Human Resources, LaTisha Daniels, if you wish to know further details.

Tom R. Benally

Stephen Van Zandt

January 17, 2024

Subject: Opting out of retirement plan

To: LaTisha Daniels <hr_ldaniels@skypark-corp>

Dear Ms. Daniels:

I would like to opt out of the retirement fund, which I am legally entitled to do under federal and state law. The details of the plan are quite generous, as the company is matching employee contributions dollar for dollar. Also, I've heard that the plan's benefits will be adjusted for inflation, which is good, and something many plans fail to do.

However, I cannot afford to invest 10% of my yearly salary at this point in my life. With two children at home and a third on the way, my wife and I need every penny we make to feed, clothe and shelter our family. Making it mandatory to pay into the plan is a bad idea, as it assumes that the only reason employees do not save for their own retirement is lack of foresight. In any event, the policy seems illegal, so I am sure you meant to say that paying into the plan is mandatory only for those who wish to benefit from it.

The timescales you have used to calculate pension eligibility are also a bit dubious. They seem more suitable to the way business was done a half-century ago than to the way it is done today, when working for one company for a lifetime is the exception rather than the norm. Still, I hope it works out well for both the company and those employees who choose to take advantage of it.

Best regards,
Stephen Van Zandt

25. **Who came up with the idea of setting up a mandatory retirement plan?**

    (A) LaTisha Daniels

    (B) Stephen Van Zandt

    (C) Tom R. Benally

    (D) Li Bachmai ⒶⒷⒸⒹ

26. **When will employees qualify to receive the pension?**

    (A) After 3 years

    (B) After 10 years

    (C) After 15 years

    (D) After 21 years ⒶⒷⒸⒹ

27. **What does Mr. Van Zandt wish to be allowed to do?**

    (A) Put his wife on the retirement plan

    (B) Take advantage of the retirement plan

    (C) Design a more suitable retirement plan

    (D) Avoid paying into the retirement plan ⒶⒷⒸⒹ

28. **In the e-mail, the word "dubious" in paragraph 3, line 2 is closest in meaning to**

    (A) reckless

    (B) doubtful

    (C) shameful

    (D) ethical ⒶⒷⒸⒹ

29. **What does Mr. Van Zandt think about the retirement plan?**

    (A) Mandatory payments for all employees are fair.

    (B) A lump sum payment to early retirees is generous.

    (C) Timescales for calculating pension eligibility are out of date.

    (D) Making withdrawals after 10 years of payments is good. ⒶⒷⒸⒹ

Media

Warm-up

Vocabulary

空欄に下から適切な語を選んで書き入れなさい。なお、動詞については原形で記されています。必要に応じて適切な形に変えなさい。

1. The negative impact of an online payment system may (   ) its advantages.
2. We found a/an (   ) in our program that caused a problem and we finally fixed it.
3. After the last shooting incident, the state government (   ) to tackle gun violence.
4. She is a/an (   ) talented singer with a beautiful voice.
5. I've been (   ) this hotel for 15 years.
6. All (   ) must be reviewed carefully by two judges.

patronize	bug	outweigh
pledge	immensely	submissions

TOEIC® Listening

Part 1 Photographs

You will hear four short statements. Look at the picture and choose the statement that best describes what you see in the picture.

1.

Ⓐ Ⓑ Ⓒ Ⓓ

2.

Ⓐ Ⓑ Ⓒ Ⓓ

Part **2** Question-Response

You will hear a question or statement and three responses. Listen carefully, and choose the best response to the question or statement.

3. Mark your answer on your answer sheet.   Ⓐ   Ⓑ   Ⓒ

4. Mark your answer on your answer sheet.   Ⓐ   Ⓑ   Ⓒ

5. Mark your answer on your answer sheet.   Ⓐ   Ⓑ   Ⓒ

6. Mark your answer on your answer sheet.   Ⓐ   Ⓑ   Ⓒ

Part **3** Conversation

You will hear a short conversation between two or more people. Listen carefully, and select the best response to each question.

7. **Who most likely is the woman?**
   (A) A candidate for a job
   (B) A salesperson
   (C) The man's co-worker
   (D) The man's supervisor   Ⓐ   Ⓑ   Ⓒ   Ⓓ

8. **What is the man's objection to the software?**
   (A) It contains some malware.
   (B) It will take too long to acclimatize the company to it.
   (C) It is way too expensive.
   (D) It requires a specialized degree.   Ⓐ   Ⓑ   Ⓒ   Ⓓ

9. **What does the woman promise the man?**
   (A) Her company's program will be quicker.
   (B) She can lower the cost a bit.
   (C) She can come back next week.
   (D) Her offered price is the lowest in the industry.   Ⓐ   Ⓑ   Ⓒ   Ⓓ

You will hear a short talk given by a single speaker. Listen carefully, and select the best response to each question.

10. **What should customers wanting information about the bug do?**

   (A) Call back at another time

   (B) Check the website

   (C) Press "1"

   (D) Press "2"

11. **Who will answer if a caller presses "1"?**

   (A) A customer service representative

   (B) A professional web designer

   (C) A salesperson

   (D) A technical expert

12. **Which customers should hold the line?**

   (A) Those who have questions about different products

   (B) Those who need an update for the HEL2200 laptop

   (C) Those who need technical help with the HEL2200 laptop

   (D) Those who want to purchase the HEL2200 laptop

Part **5** Incomplete Sentences

A word or phrase is missing in each of the sentences below. Select the best answer to complete the sentence.

13. Some governments have decided to tax sugary drinks in an effort to encourage _____ habits among their citizens.

(A) dietary   (B) healthier

(C) living   (D) neat   Ⓐ Ⓑ Ⓒ Ⓓ

14. We at Axis Technologies pledge to provide our services in the _____ confidence and with a high standard of professionalism.

(A) more strictly   (B) strict

(C) stricter   (D) strictest   Ⓐ Ⓑ Ⓒ Ⓓ

15. Harrison and Associates is looking for an experienced accountant with proven skills in bookkeeping, as _____ as corporate tax knowledge.

(A) far   (B) good

(C) long   (D) well   Ⓐ Ⓑ Ⓒ Ⓓ

16. The public's increased environmental awareness has resulted in companies taking steps to be more environmentally _____.

(A) friend   (B) friendless

(C) friendly   (D) friendship   Ⓐ Ⓑ Ⓒ Ⓓ

17. To help save the planet, consumers must be prepared to live with some inconveniences, _____ less frequent air travel.

(A) such as   (B) out of

(C) but for   (D) thanks to   Ⓐ Ⓑ Ⓒ Ⓓ

18. Some countries have introduced money made of plastic, which is said to last more than twice as _____ as regular paper bills.

(A) far   (B) long

(C) much   (D) well   Ⓐ Ⓑ Ⓒ Ⓓ

19. The speaker explained that, due to climate change, some countries are getting more rainfall, _____ other countries are experiencing longer periods of drought.

(A) instead   (B) rather

(C) whereas   (D) whether   Ⓐ Ⓑ Ⓒ Ⓓ

20. Modern consumers enjoy the power of information and expect _____ openness from the businesses they patronize.

(A) greater   (B) greatest

(C) greatly   (D) greatness   Ⓐ Ⓑ Ⓒ Ⓓ

Part **6** Text Completion

Read the text that follows. A word, phrase, or sentence is missing in parts of the text. Select the best answer to complete the text.

Questions 21-24 refer to the following promotional article.

If you've ever pondered over how to expand your reach on social media while also protecting your online privacy, ponder no more: MeWe presents a viable alternative to the problems of other platforms.

Growing _____ in the past decade, the site currently boasts around 20 million registered
       21.

users. The great thing about MeWe is that it is completely ad-free and maintains a stricter commitment to protecting users' privacy than most other big social media companies. MeWe _____ itself as "The next-gen social network," and the platform's
         22.

warm reception among the current generation of users would seem to bear that out.

If you're not already on MeWe, consider visiting mewe.com and registering for an account, which is totally free. You can join and start participating on the site within minutes. _____. From there, you can network with friends and family, _____ updates
       23.   **24.**

and photos and interacting with their content.

21. (A) immensely
    (B) relatively
    (C) scarcely
    (D) willingly
    Ⓐ Ⓑ Ⓒ Ⓓ

22. (A) insists
    (B) speculates
    (C) bills
    (D) dismisses
    Ⓐ Ⓑ Ⓒ Ⓓ

23. (A) Don't forget to pay the account fee before proceeding any further.
    (B) You could easily figure out how the website design differs from country to country.
    (C) Thus, MeWe guides you through the ins and outs of providing information online.
    (D) Be sure to fill out the information sections, add a photo and start searching for your friends.
    Ⓐ Ⓑ Ⓒ Ⓓ

24. (A) share
    (B) shared
    (C) sharing
    (D) to share
    Ⓐ Ⓑ Ⓒ Ⓓ

Read the following texts. Select the best answer for each question.

Questions 25-29 refer to the following notice, e-mail, and comments.

TRAVELING SPIRIT magazine — Submission guidelines

TRAVELING SPIRIT magazine welcomes submissions from experienced and novice writers alike. We are looking for sightseeing reviews, unique travelogues and more in-depth articles about experiences as a world traveler. Though we are a quarterly publication, we accept submissions throughout the year. Please read the following guidelines carefully before submitting your work.

Authors are limited to six submissions per year and, if chosen, only one article per author will appear in each issue.

➢ Your article should be about your own experience, not a third-person narrative about someone else's trip.

➢ We only accept articles that have not been published elsewhere. This means your article should not have appeared in print or in digital or audio format anywhere else.

➢ Article length depends on the type: reviews of specific places cannot exceed 800 words; travelogues of multi-city or multi-country trips cannot exceed 1,800 words; in-depth articles cannot exceed 3,000 words.

— Send submissions online to: editor@traveling-spirit-magazine.co.za —

John Qwelani

16 March 2023

Subject: Your submitted story

To: Melvyna Reynolds <m-reynolds@berkeley.edu>

Dear Ms. Reynolds,

Thank you for your most recent submission, "Moonlight over Buenos Aires". The editors of Traveling Spirit magazine were impressed with your description of your week in Argentina and we would like to publish it in our upcoming June issue.

I have enclosed three documents for your review and signature: an agreement of payment, a permission to publish and a photo release. The last document must be signed by you and by your traveling companion, since she is shown in one of the pictures.

I wanted to say, on a personal note, that this article was a great improvement indeed over your previous two pieces about Soweto and Sydney. It was obvious that you took our suggestions to heart and produced a truly unique piece of writing.

I look forward to receiving the documents back from you by March 20.

Yours truly,
John Qwelani
Editor

~ Comments from Our Readers ~

I was so excited to see the article about Buenos Aires in your latest Summer issue. I was there in February, just like the author was, and I participated in Carnival also. We had very different experiences, though, because I was staying in a small business hotel outside the city. I didn't lose any sleep from the noise in the streets, rather I enjoyed dancing with the locals as the music went on all night. I especially liked the pictures by Melvyna Reynolds that showed both the exciting and quieter sides of the city. Thanks to Traveling Spirit for another great story.

Paula Chisolm
Glastonbury, UK

25. **How many times a year is Traveling Spirit published?**

(A) Two

(B) Four

(C) Six

(D) Twelve   Ⓐ Ⓑ Ⓒ Ⓓ

26. **What is suggested about Ms. Reynolds' most recent article?**

(A) It is published only online.

(B) It is about traveling to Soweto.

(C) It is an in-depth travelogue.

(D) It is 800 words or fewer.   Ⓐ Ⓑ Ⓒ Ⓓ

27. **What does Mr. Qwelani imply about Ms. Reynolds' past article about Sydney?**

(A) It involved inappropriate wording.

(B) It involved good original views.

(C) It was not so intriguing.

(D) It was too long.   Ⓐ Ⓑ Ⓒ Ⓓ

28. **When did Ms. Reynolds most likely visit Argentina?**

(A) In February

(B) In March

(C) In April

(D) In October   Ⓐ Ⓑ Ⓒ Ⓓ

29. **What was Ms. Chisolm's favorite part of the article?**

(A) The lyrical writing

(B) The photographs

(C) The stories

(D) The surprise ending   Ⓐ Ⓑ Ⓒ Ⓓ

14 Health and Welfare

Warm-up

Vocabulary

空欄に下から適切な語を選んで書き入れなさい。なお、動詞については原形で記されています。また、選択肢の語は文頭に来るものも小文字で書かれています。必要に応じて適切な形に変えなさい。

1. I got my (   ) filled at a local pharmacy.
2. Overweight and (   ) are preventable by making the choice of healthier foods and regular physical activity.
3. Heavy alcohol consumption can raise your blood pressure, and increases the risk of (   ).
4. Wounds should be covered and treated by antibiotic (   ).
5. (   ) disease is a group of disorders of the heart and blood vessels.
6. She thinks that moving out of her parent's house was a (   ) in her life.

obesity	milestone	ointment
prescription	stroke	cardiovascular

TOEIC® Listening

Part 1 Photographs

You will hear four short statements. Look at the picture and choose the statement that best describes what you see in the picture.

1.

Ⓐ Ⓑ Ⓒ Ⓓ

2.

Ⓐ Ⓑ Ⓒ Ⓓ

Part 2 Question-Response

You will hear a question or statement and three responses. Listen carefully, and choose the best response to the question or statement.

3. Mark your answer on your answer sheet.   Ⓐ   Ⓑ   Ⓒ

4. Mark your answer on your answer sheet.   Ⓐ   Ⓑ   Ⓒ

5. Mark your answer on your answer sheet.   Ⓐ   Ⓑ   Ⓒ

6. Mark your answer on your answer sheet.   Ⓐ   Ⓑ   Ⓒ

Part 3 Conversation

You will hear a short conversation between two or more people. Listen carefully, and select the best response to each question.

7. **What problem are the speakers discussing?**
   (A) Complaints from parents
   (B) Late patient payments
   (C) Overcrowding
   (D) Overtime work   Ⓐ Ⓑ Ⓒ Ⓓ

8. **Look at the graphic. Which hospital do the speakers work at?**
   (A) Beeman Clinic
   (B) Central Clinic
   (C) Healthy Kids
   (D) Kids First
       Ⓐ Ⓑ Ⓒ Ⓓ

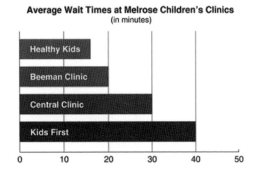

9. **What does the woman say she is going to do?**
   (A) Ask the doctor for recommendations
   (B) Contact a user of the online appointment system
   (C) Expand the waiting room
   (D) Switch to a different clinic   Ⓐ Ⓑ Ⓒ Ⓓ

You will hear a short talk given by a single speaker. Listen carefully, and select the best response to each question.

10. **What is the product used for?**

    (A) To relieve shoulder pain

    (B) To relieve headaches

    (C) To strengthen arm muscles

    (D) To strengthen back muscles   Ⓐ Ⓑ Ⓒ Ⓓ

11. **How long can the product be used before turning off automatically?**

    (A) Two hours

    (B) Three hours

    (C) Five hours

    (D) Six hours   Ⓐ Ⓑ Ⓒ Ⓓ

12. **Where can the product be purchased?**

    (A) At a drugstore

    (B) At a home improvement center

    (C) At an electronics store

    (D) At an Internet store   Ⓐ Ⓑ Ⓒ Ⓓ

Part 5 Incomplete Sentences

A word or phrase is missing in each of the sentences below. Select the best answer to complete the sentence.

13. The new prime minister promised a fair tax policy to help citizens at all income levels save money for _____ needs.
    (A) his
    (B) its
    (C) their
    (D) one's   Ⓐ Ⓑ Ⓒ Ⓓ

14. When listing skills and achievements on your résumé, think about _____ that make you valuable in the specific position you are applying for.
    (A) none
    (B) such
    (C) these
    (D) those   Ⓐ Ⓑ Ⓒ Ⓓ

15. In some countries, foreign investment in real estate, including housing, has driven up prices so much that residents _____ afford to buy homes.
    (A) cannot
    (B) do not
    (C) have not
    (D) will not   Ⓐ Ⓑ Ⓒ Ⓓ

16. The increase in the number of new jobs has been _____ the result of temporary government hiring.
    (A) large
    (B) larger
    (C) largely
    (D) largeness   Ⓐ Ⓑ Ⓒ Ⓓ

17. We didn't think we were going to _____, but we finally developed a new ointment to reduce itching caused by dryness.
    (A) come up
    (B) reach to
    (C) make it
    (D) turn it   Ⓐ Ⓑ Ⓒ Ⓓ

18. The next project meeting is _____ to take place on Friday, but we have to postpone it; Katie and Zac will be out for a meeting with their client.
    (A) inclined
    (B) supposed
    (C) about
    (D) alleged   Ⓐ Ⓑ Ⓒ Ⓓ

19. _____ outdated his research methods may be, the author's warnings on pollutant emissions are still relevant today.
    (A) However
    (B) Seldom
    (C) Rather
    (D) Throughout   Ⓐ Ⓑ Ⓒ Ⓓ

20. Even though I'm facing a difficult situation, I don't have any friends and relatives to discuss the matter with, _____ a lawyer.
    (A) unlike
    (B) despite
    (C) irrelevant of
    (D) let alone   Ⓐ Ⓑ Ⓒ Ⓓ

Part 6 Text Completion

Read the text that follows. A word, phrase, or sentence is missing in parts of the text. Select the best answer to complete the text.

Questions 21-24 refer to the following press release.

Younger, But Not Necessarily Healthier

Young people may think they are leading healthy lives, but the truth is their habits are anything but good. A new survey _____ by the American Heart Association (AHA)
                              21.
found that despite the fact that 48 percent of Americans age 18 to 24 say they enjoy healthy lifestyles, more than a third admit to engaging in behaviors that could potentially put their long-term health at risk.

This includes drinking alcohol and/or sugar-sweetened beverages, consuming too much fast food, and not eating enough fruits and vegetables.

The AHA finds this problematic since these behaviors may increase the likelihood of a stroke or cardiovascular diseases, _____ heart disease/heart attack, high blood pressure,
                        22.
obesity, high cholesterol and diabetes. America's youth should find this problematic too, since it's likely to hamper their professed desire to live to a very old age.

The AHA's conclusions are based on interviews conducted with 1,248 Americans age 18 to 44 on their _____ about health, from social influences to beliefs about health
                  23.
behaviors and risks for stroke. Responses were broken down by three demographics: young adults ages 18 to 24, 25 to 34, and 35 to 44.

_____. Only 34 percent of respondents from the 25 to 34 set, who were less likely to
    24.
eat fast food and more inclined to limit sugar-sweetened beverages and consume fruits and vegetables, said they believed they were living healthy lifestyles.

---

21. (A) conducts

(B) to conduct

(C) conducted

(D) is conducted

Ⓐ Ⓑ Ⓒ Ⓓ

22. (A) including

(B) except

(C) otherwise

(D) due to

Ⓐ Ⓑ Ⓒ Ⓓ

23. (A) influence

(B) longevity

(C) nationality

(D) attitude

Ⓐ Ⓑ Ⓒ Ⓓ

24. (A) Most people cannot judge their health condition based on the food they take in.

(B) Eating habits never change throughout a person's life.

(C) As people grew older, the AHA found, they assessed their health realistically.

(D) The way of assessment of health condition differs from person to person.

Ⓐ Ⓑ Ⓒ Ⓓ

Read the following text. Select the best answer for each question.

Questions 25-29 refer to the following article.

'Fascinated with Medicine', Cancer Research Pioneer Pushes On

Health is both a profession and a way of life for Keith Chow, a doctor and senior researcher with Arctus Medical. The 62-year-old gets up at 4:00 A.M. daily and starts his day with a jog. "I guess I'm an early riser," says Keith. "Starting the day with exercise helps keep my mind and body fresh."

Following his morning routine, Chow often puts in a 12-hour day at Arctus's laboratory in Cambridge, Massachusetts. As the head researcher for their cancer research unit, he has a lot of responsibility, but enjoys the challenge. "I've been fascinated with medicine since I was a boy," explains Chow, who moved from Guangzhou to New York to pursue a degree in pharmacology in the 1980s. "Often, I don't even notice how much time has passed at the lab, because I'm so interested in what I'm doing."

During his 30-year career with Arctus, Chow has worked on every anti-cancer drug that the company has produced. Thanks to his efforts, he has become internationally recognized as an authority on cancer therapy.

Last year, Chow reached an important personal milestone. Working in partnership with the Billington-based Cancer Research Institute, Chow played a key role in developing Mitolex, a new type of cancer drug that represents a breakthrough in treatment. The Cancer Research Institute received the prestigious Bethune Prize for their work last year, and Chow was included with the honorees. "I was just really happy to be involved in the project," remarks Chow, "and be able to do my part in the fight against cancer."

---

25. **What is the focus of Dr. Chow's work?**

    (A) Writing articles on Arctus products

    (B) Researching the effects of exercise

    (C) Developing treatment for cancer

    (D) Heading the Bethune Prize Committee   Ⓐ   Ⓑ   Ⓒ   Ⓓ

26. **Where does Dr. Chow currently work?**

    (A) Cambridge

    (B) Guangzhou

    (C) Billington

    (D) New York   Ⓐ   Ⓑ   Ⓒ   Ⓓ

27. **What is implied about Dr. Chow?**

    (A) He has been diagnosed with cancer.

    (B) He starts his job at the laboratory at 4 a.m.

    (C) He earned his degree in Guangzhou.

    (D) He is enthusiastic about his job.   Ⓐ   Ⓑ   Ⓒ   Ⓓ

28. **What most likely is Mitolex?**

    (A) A pharmaceutical company

    (B) A medical award

    (C) An innovative medication

    (D) A piece of laboratory equipment   Ⓐ   Ⓑ   Ⓒ   Ⓓ

29. **What did Dr. Chow do last year, according to the article?**

    (A) Established a new firm

    (B) Delivered an important speech

    (C) Hired a new research partner

    (D) Received an important honor   Ⓐ   Ⓑ   Ⓒ   Ⓓ

一歩上を目指す TOEIC®L&R TEST: Level 4

検印
省略

©2024 年 1 月 31 日　第 1 版発行

編著者	北尾　泰幸
	西田　晴美
	林　姿穂
	Brian Covert

発行者　　　　　小川　洋一郎

発行所　　　　　株式会社 朝日出版社

〒101-0065 東京都千代田区西神田 3-3-5
電話　東京　(03) 3239-0271
FAX　東京　(03) 3239-0479
E-mail　text-e@asahipress.com
振替口座　00140-2-46008
https://www.asahipress.com/

組版／メディアアート　製版／錦明印刷

ISBN 978-4-255-15720-7